365 Easy Soup Recipes

Simple, Delicious Soups & Stews to Warm the Heart

Cookbook Resources LLC
Highland Village, Texas

365 Easy Soup Recipes
Simple, Delicious Soups & Stews to Warm the Heart

1st Printing - March 2008
2nd Printing - December 2008
3rd Printing - November 2009

International Standard Book Number: 978-1-59769-029-4

Library of Congress Number: 2008009470

Library of Congress Cataloging-in-Publication Data

    365 easy soup recipes : simple, delicious soups & stews to warm the heart.
        p. cm.
    Previous ed.: 365 easy soups & stews, 2006.
    Includes index.
    ISBN 978-1-59769-029-4
    1. Soups. 2. Stews. 3. Quick and easy cookery. I. Cookbook Resources, LLC. II. 365 easy soups & stews. III. Title: Three hundred sixty-five easy soup recipes.
    TX757.A155 2008
    641.8'13--dc22

                       2008009470

Cover by Nancy Bohanan

Edited, Designed and Published in the United States of America by
Cookbook Resources, LLC
541 Doubletree Drive
Highland Village, Texas 75077

Toll free 866-229-2665

www.cookbookresources.com

cookbook ≡*resources*® LLC
Bringing Family and Friends to the Table

Ladle Up Comfort with Soup

Nothing says home and comfort more than a big pot of homemade soup simmering gently on the stove. Soups and stews are one of life's great comforts. They are warming, aromatic, brimming with flavor and bring back sweet memories of mom's chicken noodle soup, the one soup that always seemed to make even the worst cold vanish. There's just something about soup that makes everything seem better.

Thick or thin, hot or cold, subtle or spicy, brothy or chunky, *365 Easy Soup Recipes* has a soup to fit any mood, any every taste. From cover to cover simple delicious recipes can help make family meals into "feel-good" meals. These soups, stews, chilies and chowders are family favorites and help build family traditions.

Warm your kitchen and your heart with **Zesty Creamy Chicken Soup** on page 34, a surprisingly easy recipe for a fast chicken soup. Or try a big rich bowl of **Incredible Broccoli-Cheese Soup** on page 188. And it doesn't get any easier than **Easy Chunky Chili** on page 105, chock-full of a medley of beefy stew meat, vegetables and spices. Our collection of recipes for soups and stews makes it possible for you to ladle up a bowl of soup every day of the year!

Contents

Contents

Contents

Veggie Meatless Masterpieces

Enjoy a rich, creamy bowl of piping hot cheese soup or maybe a nice bowl loaded with big chunks of potatoes and hearty vegetables. They're wonderful.

Soup, stew, chili and chowder recipes for your slow cooker so you can come home to great taste.

Simmering Soups for Centuries

Our prehistoric ancestors, who were forced to stalk and kill their dinner before they could even think about cooking it, discovered how to mingle meats and vegetables with water before there was even a pot or kettle to cook them in! They did it for survival – a way to feed the old and toothless members of their tribes.

Fossil remains of elderly Neanderthal people were found in France with teeth worn down below gum level. They could only have been kept alive through the compassion of tribe members who found a food alternative to indigestible plants and tough meats.

Historians believe that man knew how to boil well before 6,000 B.C. when earthenware pottery was discovered. Prehistoric man found that reptile shells and animal hides made perfect vessels to boil liquid filled with fresh meat.

Evidence including residue sticking to pots indicates that our ancestors were regularly eating soup by the Bronze and Iron Ages.

The origins of the word "soup" go back to broth. Deriving from Old English, broth served over bread in a bowl was called "sop" or "sup." From this, the word "soup" evolved. In French, it is "soupe," in Spanish, "sopa," and in Dutch, "soep." In English, it's soup and we've created *365 Easy Soup Recipes* just for you.

Who's Who: Soups, Stews, Chowders and Chilies

Soups & Stews

Most of us have a pretty good idea of the difference between soups and stews. **Soups are thin and stews are thick.** But if you want to know more about these comforting dishes, read on to find out many other differences.

Soups

Soups start with liquid, usually hot water. Meats, beans and vegetables are boiled to extract the flavors of the ingredients and that is the broth or stock used as the base. As they boil they break down and mix with the liquid for a distinctive blend of flavors.

Clear Soups

Clear soups are called broth, bouillon or consomme. **Purees** are mixes of vegetables and liquid thickened by the starch in the vegetables. Other types of purees are thickened with cream, milk, eggs, rice, flour or grains.

Stews

Stews are very similar to **soups** because they are combinations of vegetables and meats cooked in a broth or stock. The ingredients are much the same as **soups**. **Stews** usually have larger pieces of meat and vegetables than do **soups**. These large pieces are boiled, covered and simmered for a long time to tenderize the ingredients.

Stews are usually served as a main course and **soups** are usually served as a first course. **Stews** are usually heartier and more filling than **soups**, but there is little difference in the popularity of both.

Chowders

Chowders are similar to stews, but mainly consist of fish or clams, potatoes and onions. New England clam **chowder** has a cream base and Manhattan clam **chowder** has a tomato base. There is also corn **chowder** with a cream base.

Chili (or is it Chile?)

Chile with an "e" refers to the many peppers available for cooking. **Chili** with an "i" refers to the state dish of Texas, where it originated. Dallas's Frank X. Tolbert, founder of the International Terlingua Chili Cook-off and chili aficionado, called **chili** "a bowl of red" to reflect the proper color of the dish.

Dedication

With a mission of helping you bring family and friends to the table, Cookbook Resources strives to make family meals and entertaining friends simple, easy and delicious.

We recognize the importance of a meal together as a means of building family bonds with memories and traditions that will be treasured for a lifetime. It is an opportunity to sit down with each other and share more than food.

This cookbook is dedicated with gratitude and respect for all those who show their love with homecooked meals, bringing family and friends to the table.

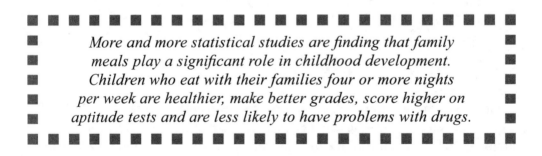

More and more statistical studies are finding that family meals play a significant role in childhood development. Children who eat with their families four or more nights per week are healthier, make better grades, score higher on aptitude tests and are less likely to have problems with drugs.

Satisfying Summer Soups

*Try one of these light
fruit or veggie soups
to refresh your senses
on a hot summer's day.*

Satisfying Summer Soups Contents

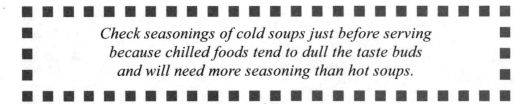

*Check seasonings of cold soups just before serving
because chilled foods tend to dull the taste buds
and will need more seasoning than hot soups.*

Cold Peach Soup

This is a beautiful and delicious soup to serve as a first course at a ladies' luncheon or gathering of friends.

1½ pounds fresh peaches, peeled, sliced	680 g
1 (8 ounce) carton sour cream	230 g
1 (8 ounce) carton peach yogurt	230 g
2½ cups orange juice	625 ml
1 tablespoon lemon juice	15 ml
3 tablespoons sugar	40 g

- Puree peaches in blender or food processor until smooth. Add sour cream, yogurt, orange juice and lemon juice and process until they blend well. Stir in sugar, cover and refrigerate for at least 2 hours. Serves 8.

Edna Earle's Cold Peach Soup

This is delicious for summer luncheons with vegetables or chicken-salad sandwiches.

2 pounds peaches	910 g
1 tablespoon lemon juice	15 ml
3 tablespoons quick-cooking tapioca	50 g
3 tablespoons sugar	40 g
1 (6 ounce) can frozen orange juice concentrate	170 g

- Puree peaches with lemon juice and set aside. Combine tapioca, sugar, a little salt and 1 cup (250 ml) water in saucepan. Heat to full boil and stir constantly until mixture thickens.

- Transfer to medium bowl. Stir in orange juice until it melts. Add 1½ cups (375 ml) water and stir until smooth. Mix in pureed peaches, cover and refrigerate. Serve cold. Serves 8.

TIP· Make this soup ahead of time so it has time to chill.

Luncheon Fruit Soup

¾ cup sugar	150 g
4 tablespoons quick-cooking tapioca	70 g
¼ teaspoon ground cinnamon	1 ml
1 (6 ounce) can frozen orange juice concentrate, thawed	170 g
2 cups frozen, sliced peaches, thawed	310 g
1 (15 ounce) can pear slices with juice	425 g
1 (8 ounce) can crushed pineapple with juice	230 g
1 (16 ounce) package sliced, sweetened strawberries, thawed	455 g

- Combine sugar, tapioca, cinnamon and 3 cups (750 ml) water in large saucepan. Cook over medium heat and stir constantly for about 10 minutes or until mixture thickens. Remove from heat and pour in orange juice concentrate.

- Cut peaches and pears into bite-size pieces. Stir peaches, pears, pineapple and strawberries into tapioca-orange juice mixture. Cover and refrigerate for at least 2 hours. Serves 8.

Pat's Chilled Strawberry Soup

2 (10 ounce) packages
   strawberries in
   syrup   **2 (280 g)**
½ cup cranberries **50 g**
2 (8 ounce) cartons
   strawberry yogurt **2 (230 g)**

- Combine all ingredients in blender and mix until smooth.

- Refrigerate for 1 to 2 hours before serving. Serves 4.

Cold Strawberry Soup

2¼ cups strawberries   **405 g**
⅓ cup sugar   **70 g**
½ cup sour cream   **120 g**
½ cup whipping cream **125 ml**
½ cup light red wine   **125 ml**

- Puree strawberries and sugar in blender. Pour into pitcher, stir in sour cream and whipping cream and blend well.

- Add red wine and 1¼ cups (310 ml) water. Stir and refrigerate before serving. Serves 4 to 6.

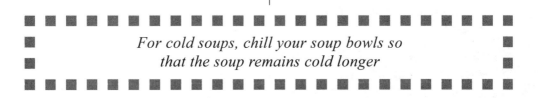

*For cold soups, chill your soup bowls so
that the soup remains cold longer*

Chilled Summertime Soup

3 cups chilled, cubed fresh cantaloupe, divided	530 g
3 cups chilled, cubed fresh honeydew melon	530 g
2 cups chilled, fresh orange juice	500 ml
2 cups chilled, white wine or champagne	500 ml
¼ cup chilled, fresh lime juice	60 ml
3 tablespoons honey	65 g

- Puree 2 cups (355 g) cantaloupe in food processor or blender and pour into large bowl. Puree honeydew melon and combine with pureed cantaloupe, orange juice, white wine and lime juice.

- Pour in honey and mix well. Chop remaining cantaloupe and add to bowl. Serve immediately. Serves 8.

TIP: Fresh mint as garnish is always a nice touch.

Strawberry-Orange Soup

1½ cups fresh strawberries	270 g
1 cup orange juice	250 ml
¼ cup honey	85 g
½ cup sour cream	120 g
½ cup white wine	125 ml

- Combine all ingredients in blender and puree.

- Chill thoroughly. Stir before pouring into individual soup bowls. Serves 4.

Chilled Yogurt Soups

Here are two light, chilled soups that are unusually good. Yogurt has a unique flavor and gives soups a delicious, tangy taste. Both of these soups are prepared the same way, but one uses cucumber and one uses avocados.

Chilled Yogurt Soup with Cucumbers

4 cucumbers, peeled,
   seeded, divided
3 cups plain yogurt   680 g
1 tablespoon minced
   onion   15 ml

- Place 3 cucumbers, yogurt and onion in food processor or blender and process until just smooth. Add a little salt, cover and refrigerate for several hours.

- Chill soup bowls at the same time and pour soup into bowls when ready to serve. Thinly slice remaining cucumber and garnish soup with several slices. Serves 4.

Chilled Yogurt Soup with Avocados

4 ripe avocados, peeled,
   seeded, divided
3 cups plain yogurt   680 g
1 tablespoon minced
   onion   15 ml

- Place 3 avocados, yogurt and onion in food processor or blender and process until just smooth. Add a little salt, cover and refrigerate for several hours.

- Chill soup bowls at the same time and pour soup into bowls when ready to serve. Thinly slice remaining avocado and garnish soup with several slices. Serves 4.

Summer Breeze Raspberry Soup

3½ cups fresh raspberries 430 g
1 cup rose wine   250 ml
¾ cup sugar   150 g
1 (8 ounce) carton sour
    cream   230 g

- Mash raspberries in bowl, mix in blender and strain to remove seeds. Add enough water to make 3½ cups (875 ml). Place raspberry mixture, wine, sugar and a little salt in saucepan.

- Bring to a boil, reduce heat, cover and simmer for 5 minutes. Cool, add sour cream and stir until it blends thoroughly. Refrigerate for about 4 hours. Serves 6.

Easy Gazpacho

2 (28 ounce) cans
    diced tomatoes   2 (795 g)
1 seedless cucumber,
    peeled, cubed
1 cup chopped red
    onion   160 g
1 cup chopped celery   100 g
2 serrano chile
    peppers, seeded,
    coarsely chopped

- Work in batches to combine all ingredients plus a little salt and pepper in food processor and pulse until mixture is thick.

- Garnish with several lemon slices, if desired. Serves 8.

TIP: Wear rubber gloves when removing seeds from peppers.

White Gazpacho

¼ cup packed parsley
    leaves   60 ml
3 cloves garlic,
    chopped
1 teaspoon dried
    basil   5 ml
1 teaspoon dried
    oregano   5 ml
3 seedless cucumbers,
    peeled, chopped
1 green bell pepper,
    seeded, quartered
1 white onion,
    quartered
2 (8 ounce) cartons
    plain yogurt   2 (230 g)
2 (14 ounce) cans
    chicken broth   2 (400 g)
2 tablespoons lemon
    juice   30 ml
Hot sauce

- Finely chop parsley and add garlic, basil and oregano in bowl. Place cucumbers, green pepper and onion in blender, process until coarsely chopped and add parsley mixture.

- Stir in yogurt, broth, lemon juice and ½ teaspoon (2 ml) each of salt and pepper and mix well. Season to taste with hot sauce and refrigerate. Serves 6.

Rio Grande Gazpacho

This spicy vegetable soup made from a puree of raw vegetables is served cold and is great in the summer.

1 cucumber, peeled, seeded, quartered	
1 bell pepper, seeded, quartered	
½ onion, quartered	
1 teaspoon minced garlic	5 ml
2 teaspoons chopped fresh parsley	10 ml
3¼ cups tomato juice, divided	810 ml
1 pound tomatoes, peeled, quartered, cored	455 g
¼ cup sliced pimento-stuffed olives	30 g
3 tablespoons red wine vinegar	45 ml
1 tablespoons olive oil	15 ml
½ teaspoon ground cumin	2 ml
½ teaspoon oregano	2 ml
2 teaspoons hot sauce	10 ml

- Combine cucumber, bell pepper, onion, garlic, parsley and 2 cups (500 ml) tomato juice in blender. Process until vegetables are coarsely chopped. Add tomatoes and process again until vegetables are finely chopped.

- Pour into medium container with tight lid. Stir in olives, wine vinegar, olive oil, ½ teaspoon (2 ml) salt, cumin, oregano and hot sauce.

- Stir in remaining tomato juice, cover and refrigerate for 24 hours. Serve cold. Serves 6.

Gazpacho

2 large ripe tomatoes, chopped, drained	
1 yellow onion, finely chopped	
1 seedless cucumber, peeled, chopped	
1 teaspoon minced garlic	5 ml
1 (7 ounce) jar roasted red bell peppers, drained	200 g
1 (48 ounce) can tomato juice	1.4 L
¼ cup lime juice	60 ml
¼ cup red wine vinegar	60 ml
2 tablespoons olive oil	30 ml
½ teaspoon sugar	2 ml
1 teaspoon hot sauce	5 ml

- Process tomatoes, onion, cucumber, garlic and roasted bell peppers in food processor or blender.

- Stir puree, tomato juice, lime juice, vinegar, oil, sugar, hot sauce and a little salt and pepper. Cover and refrigerate for at least 4 hours. Serves 8.

Cucumber Dill Soup

3 medium cucumbers, peeled, seeded, cubed	
1 (14 ounce) can chicken broth, divided	400 g
1 (8 ounce) carton sour cream	230 g
3 tablespoons fresh chives, minced	45 ml
2 teaspoons fresh dill, minced	10 ml

- Combine cucumbers, 1 cup (250 ml) chicken broth and a little salt in blender. Cover and process until smooth. Transfer to medium bowl and stir in remaining chicken broth.

- Whisk in sour cream, chives and dill. Cover and refrigerate before serving. Garnish with a sprig of dill. Serves 6.

Vichyssoise

¼ **cup (½ stick)**
 butter   **60 g**
1 onion, chopped
3 medium potatoes,
 peeled, sliced
2 (14 ounce) cans
 chicken broth   **2 (400 g)**
2 cups milk   **500 ml**
1 (8 ounce) carton
 whipping cream   **250 ml**

- Melt butter and saute onion in large soup pot. Add sliced potatoes and chicken broth and bring to boil. Reduce heat and simmer about 35 minutes or until potatoes are tender.

- Place about half soup mixture in blender, process until smooth and return to soup pot. Repeat with remaining soup mixture. Stir constantly and add milk, ½ teaspoon (2 ml) pepper and a little salt. Cover and heat on medium until thoroughly hot. Cool.

- Stir in whipping cream, cover and refrigerate. Serve in chilled individual bowls or cover and refrigerate up to 24 hours. Serves 6.

TIP: A parsley garnish is a nice touch, but not a "must".

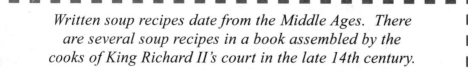

Written soup recipes date from the Middle Ages. There are several soup recipes in a book assembled by the cooks of King Richard II's court in the late 14th century.

Artichoke Soup

3 tablespoons butter	40 g
2 tablespoons finely minced green onions	10 g
1½ tablespoons flour	10 g
2 (14 ounce) cans chicken broth	2 (400 g)
1 (16 ounce) can artichoke bottoms, drained	455 g
1 cup half-and-half cream	250 ml

- Melt butter in large saucepan and saute green onions. Stir in flour and cook for 3 minutes. Slowly add broth, stir constantly and cook on medium heat until mixture thickens.

- Puree artichokes in blender and stir into broth mixture plus a little salt and pepper. Add half-and-half cream and heat just until soup is thoroughly hot.

- This soup may be served hot or cold; therefore, when serving cold, do not heat after adding cream. Refrigerate for 2 hours before serving. Serves 6.

Asparagus Chiller

1 (10 ounce) can cream of asparagus soup	280 g
⅔ cup sour cream	160 g
½ cup finely chopped cucumber	60 g
2 tablespoons chopped red onion	20 g

- Blend soup, sour cream and ¾ soup can water in bowl. Stir in cucumber and onion.

- Refrigerate for at least 4 hours and serve in chilled bowls. Serves 4.

Chilled Cucumber Soup

2 seedless cucumbers, peeled	
½ cup buttermilk, divided*	125 ml
½ cup sour cream	120 g
2 teaspoons white vinegar	10 ml
1 teaspoon olive oil	5 ml
1 teaspoon sugar	5 ml
½ teaspoon dried dill, crumbled	2 ml

- Coarsely chop cucumbers and place cucumbers and ¼ cup (60 ml) buttermilk in blender or food processor and puree. Transfer to bowl and whisk in remaining ingredients with a little salt and pepper.

- Cover bowl, refrigerate for 30 minutes and stir occasionally. Serve in chilled bowls. Serves 4.

TIP: To make buttermilk, mix 1 cup (250 ml) milk with 1 tablespoon (15 ml) lemon juice or vinegar and let milk stand for about 10 minutes.

Easy Yogurt-Cucumber Chiller

1 (1 pint) carton plain yogurt	500 ml
1 (10 ounce) can chicken broth	280 g
1 lemon	
¾ cup peeled, seeded, grated cucumber	90 g
¼ cup whipping cream	60 ml
1 teaspoon finely chopped green onion with tops	5 ml
½ teaspoon chopped fresh dill	2 ml

- Add yogurt to chicken broth in large bowl and mix well. Cut lemon in half and squeeze 1 teaspoon (5 ml) juice into broth mixture. Cut very thin slices from other half and refrigerate.

- Add remaining ingredients with a little salt and pepper and stir until soup blends well. Refrigerate for at least 4 hours. Before serving, place 1 slice lemon on top of each serving. Serves 8.

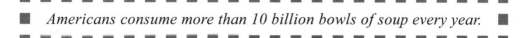

Americans consume more than 10 billion bowls of soup every year.

Quick Borscht

1 (15 ounce) jar whole
  red beets   425 g
1 (14 ounce) can beef
  broth   400 g
¼ cup sour cream   60 g

- Drain beets and save liquid.
  Chop beets and combine
  with beet liquid and broth in
  saucepan. Heat for 10 minutes.

- Refrigerate and serve with
  dollop of sour cream. Serves 4.

Creamy Cucumber Soup

2 seedless cucumbers,
  peeled, coarsely
  chopped
2 green onions, coarsely
  chopped
1 tablespoon lemon juice   15 ml
1 (1 pint) carton half-
  and-half cream   500 ml
1 (8 ounce) carton sour
  cream   230 g
1 teaspoon dried dill weed 5 ml

- Process cucumbers, onions and
  lemon juice in blender until
  mixture is smooth. Transfer
  pureed mixture to bowl with lid.

- Gently stir in half-and-half
  cream, sour cream, dill weed,
  1 teaspoon (5 ml) salt and
  ½ teaspoon (2 ml) pepper. Add
  a dash of hot sauce, if you like.

- Cover and refrigerate for several
  hours before serving. Stir
  mixture well before serving in
  soup bowls. Serves 6.

Sweet Carrot Soup

1 (16 ounce) package	
shredded carrots	455 g
1 cup orange juice	250 ml
1 cup apricot nectar	250 ml
¼ cup lemon juice	60 ml
⅓ cup honey	115 g
⅓ cup sour cream	80 g

- Combine carrots, orange juice, apricot nectar and ½ cup (125 ml) water in large saucepan. Bring to boil, reduce heat and simmer for 20 minutes.

- Add lemon juice, honey and sour cream and stir well. Serve soup at room temperature or chilled. Serves 6.

Fresh Avocado Soup

3 ripe avocados	
4 tablespoons fresh	
lemon juice	60 ml
1 (10 ounce) can chicken	
broth	280 g
1 (8 ounce) carton plain	
yogurt	230 g
Chopped chives	

- Peel avocados, remove seeds and cut into pieces. Immediately put avocados, lemon juice, broth and yogurt into blender and process until smooth.

- Add a little salt and pepper and refrigerate for several hours. Serve in soup bowls with chopped chives on top. Serves 4 to 6.

Avocado-Cream Soup

4 large, ripe avocados,
    peeled, diced,
    divided
1½ cups whipping
    cream, divided   375 ml
2 (14 ounce) cans
    chicken broth   2 (400 g)
¼ cup dry sherry   60 ml

- Puree 2 avocados and half whipping cream in blender. Repeat with remaining avocados and cream.

- Bring chicken broth to boil, reduce heat and stir in avocado puree. Add 1 teaspoon (5 ml) salt and sherry and chill thoroughly. Serve in chilled soup bowls. Serves 6.

Chilled Squash Soup

2 pounds yellow squash,
    thinly sliced   910 g
1 onion, chopped
1 (14 ounce) can chicken
    broth   400 g
1 (8 ounce) package
    cream cheese,
    softened   230 g

- Combine squash, onion and broth in saucepan and bring to boil. Cover, reduce heat and simmer for 10 minutes or until tender. Set aside until slightly cool.

- Spoon half squash mixture and half cream cheese into blender. Process until smooth and stop once to scrape down sides. Repeat procedure.

- Stir in a little salt and pepper and refrigerate. Serves 6.

Chicken Chill Chasers

*Simple, feel-better recipes
for soups, stews, chilies
and chowders to chase
away the blahs.*

Chicken Chill Chasers Contents

County's Best Chicken Soup

4 boneless, skinless
   chicken breast
   halves
3 (14 ounce) cans
   chicken broth   3 (400 g)
2 tablespoons butter   30 g
3 medium new (red)
   potatoes, cut into
   wedges
2 ribs celery, chopped
1 carrot, peeled,
   shredded
1 (10 ounce) package
   frozen green peas   280 g
1 (10 ounce) package
   frozen corn   280 g
1½ cups buttermilk*   375 ml
½ cup flour   60 g
½ teaspoon cayenne
   pepper   2 ml
1 teaspoon
   Worcestershire
   sauce   5 ml

- Bring chicken and broth to a boil in large saucepan and cook for 10 minutes or until done. Remove chicken with slotted spoon and save broth. Cut chicken into bite-size pieces.

- Melt butter in soup pot, add potatoes and cook for about 10 minutes. Add reserved broth, chicken, celery, carrot, peas and corn and simmer for 30 minutes.

- Stir buttermilk and flour until smooth, add to chicken-potato mixture and cook, stirring constantly for 5 minutes. Stir in cayenne pepper and Worcestershire sauce. Serves 8.

*TIP: To make buttermilk, mix 1 cup (250 ml) milk with 1 tablespoon (15 ml) lemon juice or vinegar and let milk stand for about 10 minutes.

All-American Soup

3 boneless, skinless
    chicken breast
    halves, cut into strips
1 onion, chopped
Olive oil
1 (10 ounce) can
    tomatoes and
    green chilies   280 g
2 (14 ounce) cans
    chicken broth   2 (400 g)
3 large baking
    potatoes, peeled,
    cubed
1 (10 ounce) can
    cream of celery
    soup   280 g
1 cup milk   250 ml
1 teaspoon dried
    basil   5 ml
1 (8 ounce) package
    shredded
    Velveeta® cheese   230 g
½ cup sour cream   120 g

- Brown and cook chicken strips and onion in large saucepan with a little oil for about 10 minutes.

- Add tomatoes and green chilies, chicken broth and cubed potatoes. Boil and cook for 15 minutes or until potatoes are tender.

- Stir in soup, milk, basil and 1 teaspoon (5 ml) salt. Cook on medium heat and stir constantly until thoroughly hot.

- Stir in cheese until cheese melts. Remove from heat and stir in sour cream. Serves 8.

Creamy Broccoli-Rice Soup

1 (6 ounce) package
chicken and wild
rice mix   170 g
1 (10 ounce) package
frozen chopped
broccoli   280 g
2 (10 ounce) cans
cream of chicken
soup   2 (280 g)
1 (12 ounce) can
chicken breast
chunks   340 g

- Combine rice mix, contents of seasoning packet and 5 cups (1.2 L) water in soup pot. Bring to boil, reduce heat and simmer for 15 minutes.

- Stir in broccoli, chicken soup and chicken. Cover and simmer for additional 5 minutes. Serves 8.

Chicken-Veggie Soup

1 (32 ounce) carton
chicken broth   910 g
2 small carrots, thinly
sliced
1 rib celery, diced
1 baby leek, halved
lengthwise, sliced
1 (8 ounce) can green
peas   230 g
1 cup cooked rice   165 g
1 cup cooked, sliced
chicken   140 g
2 teaspoons chopped
fresh tarragon   10 ml

- Pour stock in large saucepan and add carrots, celery and leek. Bring to boil, reduce heat and simmer, partially covered for 10 minutes.

- Stir in peas, rice and chicken and continue cooking for 10 to 15 minutes or until vegetables are tender. Add chopped tarragon and a little salt and pepper. Serves 8.

Zesty Creamy Chicken Soup

This is a really easy way to whip up a fast chicken soup.

2 tablespoons butter	**30 g**
½ onion, finely chopped	
1 carrot, grated	
1 (10 ounce) can cream	
of celery soup	**280 g**
1 (10 ounce) can cream	
of mushroom soup	**280 g**
1 (10 ounce) can cream	
of chicken soup	**280 g**
1 (14 ounce) can chicken	
broth	**400 g**
2 soup cans milk	
1 tablespoon dried	
parsley flakes	**15 ml**
¼ teaspoon garlic powder	**1 ml**
1 (16 ounce) package,	
cubed Mexican	
Velveeta® cheese	**455 g**
4 boneless, skinless	
chicken breast halves,	
cooked, diced	

- Melt butter in large saucepan or roasting pan and saute onion and carrots for 10 minutes, but do not brown. Add remaining ingredients and heat but do not boil.

- Reduce heat to low, cook until cheese melts and stir constantly. Serve piping hot. Serves 8.

TIP: This is really the "easy" way to make chicken soup and if you are in an absolute rush, you could even use 2 (12 ounces/340 g) cans chicken. Leftover turkey could be substituted for chicken.

Cheesy Chicken Soup

1 (10 ounce) can fiesta
    nacho cheese soup   280 g
1 (10 ounce) can cream
    of chicken soup   280 g
1 soup can milk
1 (12 ounce) can chicken
    breasts with liquid   340 g

- Mix all ingredients in saucepan on medium heat and stir until thoroughly hot. Serve hot. Serves 4 to 6.

Chicken-Rice Soup with Green Chilies

8 boneless, skinless
    chicken breast
    halves, cooked
2 (14 ounce) cans
    chicken broth   2 (400 g)
1 cup chopped celery   100 g
1 cup rice   185 g
2 - 4 large fresh,
    green chilies,
    seeded, chopped

- Cut cooked chicken into small pieces and place in large saucepan.

- Add chicken broth, celery, rice, green chilies, 1 teaspoon (5 ml) salt and ¼ teaspoon (1 ml) pepper and simmer for about 35 minutes or until rice is tender. Serves 6.

Chicken and Rice Gumbo

3 (14 ounce) cans
    chicken broth   **3 (400 g)**
1 pound boneless,
    skinless chicken
    breasts, cubed   **455 g**
2 (15 ounce) cans
    whole kernel corn,
    drained   **2 (425 g)**
2 (15 ounce) cans
    stewed tomatoes
    with liquid   **2 (425 g)**
¾ cup white rice   **140 g**
1 teaspoon Cajun
    seasoning   **5 ml**
2 (10 ounce) packages
    frozen okra,
    thawed, chopped   **2 (280 g)**

- Combine chicken broth and chicken in soup pot and cook on high heat for 15 minutes.

- Add remaining ingredients and 1 teaspoon (5 ml) pepper and bring to boil. Reduce heat and simmer for 30 minutes or until rice is done. Serves 8.

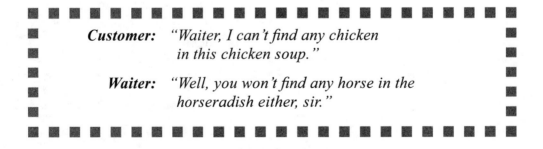

Customer: *"Waiter, I can't find any chicken in this chicken soup."*

Waiter: *"Well, you won't find any horse in the horseradish either, sir."*

Creamy Chicken-Spinach Soup

1 (9 ounce) package
  refrigerated cheese
  tortellini   255 g
2 (14 ounce) cans
  chicken broth,
  divided   2 (400 g)
1 (10 ounce) can
  cream of chicken
  soup   280 g
1 (12 ounce) can white
  chicken meat with
  liquid   340 g
1 (10 ounce) package
  frozen chopped
  spinach   280 g
2 cups milk   500 ml
½ teaspoon dried
  thyme   2 ml

- Cook tortellini in soup pot with 1 can chicken broth according to package directions.

- Stir in remaining can broth, soup, chicken, spinach, milk, 1 teaspoon (5 ml) salt, ½ teaspoon (2 ml) pepper and thyme.

- Bring to boil, reduce heat to low and simmer for 10 minutes. Serves 8.

Cold Night Bean Soup

1½ cups dried navy beans	395 g
3 (14 ounce) cans chicken broth	3 (400 g)
4 tablespoons (½ stick) butter	55 g
1 onion, chopped	
1 clove garlic, minced	
3 cups chopped, cooked chicken	420 g
1 (4 ounce) can chopped green chilies	115 g
1½ teaspoons ground cumin	7 ml
½ teaspoon cayenne pepper	2 ml
Shredded Monterey Jack cheese	

- Sort and wash beans and place in soup pot. Cover with water 2 inches (5 cm) above beans and soak overnight.

- Drain beans and add broth, butter, 1 cup (250 ml) water, onion and garlic. Bring to boil, reduce heat and cover. Simmer for 2 hours and stir occasionally. Add more water if needed.

- With potato masher, mash half beans. Add chicken, green chilies, cumin and cayenne pepper. Bring to boil, reduce heat and cover. Simmer for additional 30 minutes.

- When ready to serve, spoon in bowls and top with 1 to 2 tablespoons (10 to 15 g) cheese. Serves 8.

Quick Chicken-Noodle Soup

2 (14 ounce) cans
  chicken broth   2 (400 g)
2 boneless, skinless
  chicken breast
  halves, cubed
1 (8 ounce) can sliced
  carrots, drained   230 g
2 ribs celery, sliced
½ (8 ounce) package
  medium egg
  noodles   ½ (230 g)

- Combine broth, chicken, carrots, celery and generous dash of pepper in large saucepan. Boil and cook for 3 minutes.

- Stir in noodles, reduce heat and cook for 10 minutes or until noodles are done; stir often. Serves 4 to 6.

Speedy Gonzalez Soup

1 (12 ounce) can chicken
  with liquid   340 g
1 (14 ounce) can chicken
  broth   400 g
1 (16 ounce) jar mild
  thick-and-chunky
  salsa   455 g
1 (15 ounce) can
  ranch-style beans   425 g

- Combine chicken, broth, salsa and beans in large saucepan.

- Bring to boil, reduce heat and simmer for 15 minutes. Serves 6.

TIP: If you have 1 (15 ounce/425 g) can whole kernel corn, add it for a crunchy texture.

Feel-Better Chicken-Noodle Soup

1 (3 ounce) package chicken-flavored ramen noodles, broken	85 g
1 (10 ounce) package frozen green peas, thawed	280 g
2 teaspoons butter	10 ml
1 (4 ounce) jar sliced mushrooms, drained	115 g
3 cups cooked, cubed chicken	420 g

- Heat 2¼ cups (560 ml) water in large saucepan to boiling.

- Add ramen noodles, contents of seasoning packet, peas and butter. Heat to boiling, reduce heat to medium and cook for about 5 minutes.

- Stir in mushrooms and chicken and continue cooking over low heat until all ingredients heat through. To serve, spoon into serving bowls. Serves 6.

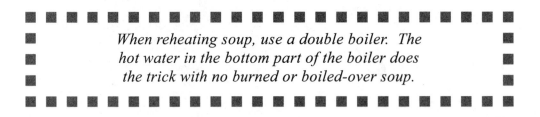

When reheating soup, use a double boiler. The hot water in the bottom part of the boiler does the trick with no burned or boiled-over soup.

Chicken-Veggie Surprise

3 (14 ounce) cans
   chicken broth   3 (400 g)
1 (15 ounce) can
   sliced carrots,
   drained   425 g
1 (15 ounce) can peas,
   drained   425 g
1 red bell pepper,
   seeded, chopped
1 teaspoon dried
   tarragon   5 ml
½ pound boneless,
   skinless chicken
   breasts, cooked,
   cut into strips   230 g
1 (16 ounce) package
   frozen broccoli
   florets   455 g
4 ounces thin egg
   noodles   115 g

- Combine broth, carrots, peas, bell pepper, tarragon and 1 teaspoon (5 ml) salt in large soup pot.

- Bring to boil, reduce heat and simmer for 5 minutes.

- Add chicken strips and broccoli and cook for an additional 10 minutes.

- Stir in noodles, bring to boil, reduce heat to medium and cook for 10 minutes or until noodles are tender. Serves 8.

Tempting Tortilla Soup

Don't let the number of ingredients keep you from serving this. It's really easy.

3 large boneless,
   skinless chicken
   breast halves,
   cooked, cubed
1 (10 ounce) package
   frozen corn,
   thawed   280 g
1 onion, chopped
3 (14 ounce) cans
   chicken broth   3 (400 g)
2 (10 ounce) cans
   tomatoes and
   green chilies   2 (280 g)
2 teaspoons ground
   cumin   10 ml
1 teaspoon chili
   powder   5 ml
1 clove garlic, minced
6 corn tortillas

- Combine all ingredients except tortillas in large soup pot. Bring to boil, reduce heat and simmer for 35 minutes.

- Preheat oven to 350º (175° C).

- While soup simmers, cut tortillas into 1-inch (2.5 cm) strips and place on baking sheet. Bake for about 5 minutes or until crisp. Serve tortilla strips with each serving of soup. Serves 6.

La Placita Enchilada Soup

6 boneless, skinless chicken breast halves	
½ cup (1 stick) butter	115 g
2 cloves garlic, minced	
1 onion, minced	
⅓ cup flour	40 g
1 (15 ounce) can Mexican stewed tomatoes, chopped	425 g
1 (7 ounce) can chopped green chilies	200 g
1 (1 pint) carton sour cream	480 g
1 (8 ounce) package shredded cheddar cheese	230 g

- Cook chicken with 12 cups (3 L) water in large saucepan until tender. Reserve broth, cube chicken and set aside. Melt butter in large roasting pan and cook garlic and onion until tender.

- Add 1 teaspoon (5 ml) salt to flour in bowl, slowly pour flour into butter mixture and stir constantly to dissolve all lumps.

- Continue stirring and slowly pour in reserved chicken broth. Cook until soup thickens to right consistency.

- Add chicken, tomatoes, green chilies and sour cream. Mix well and heat. Serve in individual bowls and sprinkle with cheese. Serves 6.

Screamin' Jalapeno Soup

3 carrots, peeled, diced
2 ribs celery, chopped
1 green bell pepper,
    seeded, chopped
6 tablespoons
    (¾ stick) butter,
    divided   85 g
2 (14 ounce) cans
    chicken broth   2 (400 g)
3 cups cooked,
    shredded chicken   420 g
3 - 5 jalapenos,
    seeded, chopped
¼ cup flour   30 g
1½ teaspoons ground
    cumin   7 ml
1 (1 pint) carton
    whipping cream   500 ml

- Combine carrots, celery and bell pepper in large skillet and saute in 4 tablespoons (55 g) butter.

- Transfer to large soup pot and add chicken broth, shredded chicken and jalapenos (3 for medium heat and 5 for serious heat). Bring to boil, reduce heat and simmer for about 30 minutes.

- In same skillet, melt remaining 2 tablespoons (30 g) butter and add flour and cumin.

- Heat mixture on medium-low heat, stirring constantly, to make a light brown roux.

- Stir in whipping cream, stirring constantly, but do not boil.

- Pour cream mixture into vegetable-chicken mixture and heat on medium, stirring constantly, just until mixture thickens. Serves 6.

TIP: *If you like it extra hot, leave the seeds and veins in the jalapenos. Wear rubber gloves when removing seeds from jalapenos.*

Sopa de Lima

*This is a traditional lime
and tortilla soup.*

**4 - 6 boneless, skinless
    chicken breast halves**
1 onion, minced
**1 red bell pepper,
    seeded, chopped**
2 cloves garlic, minced
2 tablespoons canola oil   30 ml
6 limes, divided
**3 fresh jalapeno or
    serrano chiles,
    seeded, minced**
**3 tomatoes, peeled,
    seeded, chopped**
**1 (32 ounce) carton
    chicken broth   910 g**
8 corn tortillas

- Cook chicken, chop into small pieces in skillet and set aside. Cook onion, bell pepper and garlic in saucepan with hot oil until onion is translucent.

- Cut 1 lime in half, juice lime and place 2 rind shells into saucepan. Slice remaining limes and set aside.

- Add chiles, tomatoes and broth, simmer for about 10 minutes and discard lime shells. Season chicken with a little salt and pepper and add to saucepan.

- Cut tortillas in half and slice into narrow strips. Heat oil in large skillet and cook tortilla strips until crispy. Drain on paper towel and place in warm oven until all strips cook.

- Taste soup for seasonings. Pour into individual soup bowls and place lime slice and tortilla strips on top. Serves 8.

*TIP: Wear rubber gloves
    when removing seeds
    from jalapenos.*

Seaside Soup Cancun

4 (14 ounce) cans
    chicken broth   4 (400 g)
1 bunch fresh
    cilantro, coarsely
    chopped
3 boneless, skinless
    chicken breast halves
1 ear fresh corn, cut
    into 6 rounds
1 tablespoon ground
    cumin   15 ml
2 tablespoons butter   30 g
2 onions, chopped
1 red bell pepper,
    thinly sliced
1 clove garlic, minced
2 tomatoes, chopped
1 poblano chile, seeded,
    chopped
½ teaspoon sugar   2 ml
4 corn tortillas
Olive oil
4 tablespoons lime
    juice   60 ml
Sour cream

- Bring chicken broth to boil in large saucepan over high heat. Add cilantro, chicken, corn and cumin. Cook until chicken and corn are done, for about 15 minutes.

- Melt butter in skillet and add onion, bell pepper, garlic and tomatoes. Cook, stirring frequently for about 10 minutes.

- Cut chile into ¼-inch (6 mm) rounds and add to skillet. Add tomato mixture and sugar to chicken mixture. Cook for additional 10 minutes.

- Cut tortillas into thin strips, fry in skillet with oil until crispy and drain. Stir in lime juice and pour soup into serving bowls. Garnish with strips of fried tortillas and 1 heaping tablespoon (15 ml) sour cream. Serves 8.

Fast Fiesta Soup

1 (15 ounce) can
   Mexican stewed
   tomatoes   425 g
1 (15 ounce) can
   whole kernel corn 425 g
1 (15 ounce) can pinto
   beans with liquid 425 g
2 (14 ounce) cans
   chicken broth   2 (400 g)
1 (10 ounce) can
   fiesta nacho soup 280 g
1 (12 ounce) can
   chicken breast
   with liquid   340 g

- Combine tomatoes, corn, beans, broth and nacho soup in large soup pot, heat for 10 minutes over medium heat and mix well.

- Stir in chicken with liquid and heat until thoroughly hot. Serves 6.

Oriental Chicken-Noodle Soup

1 (3 ounce) package
   chicken-flavor
   ramen noodles   85 g
1 rotisserie chicken,
   boned, skinned, cubed
2 medium stalks bok choy
   with leaves, thinly
   sliced
1 (8 ounce) can sliced
   carrots, drained   230 g
1 red bell pepper,
   seeded, chopped

- Break apart noodles, place in 3 cups (750 ml) water and heat in soup pot. Stir in chicken, bok choy, carrots and bell pepper.

- Bring to boil, reduce heat and simmer for 3 minutes; stir occasionally. Stir in flavor packet from noodles and serve immediately. Serves 8.

Zesty Chicken Stew

8 boneless, skinless
chicken thighs
¼ cup flour   **30 g**
3 tablespoons olive oil   **45 ml**
¾ teaspoon dried oregano   **4 ml**
¾ teaspoon dried basil   **4 ml**
1 large onion, chopped
1 cup white cooking wine   **250 ml**
1 (14 ounce) can chicken
broth   **400 g**
3 medium new (red)
potatoes, peeled, diced
1 (15 ounce) can diced
tomatoes, drained   **425 g**
1 (8 ounce) can sliced
carrots, drained   **230 g**
3 tablespoons chopped
fresh cilantro   **45 ml**
Brown rice, cooked

- Lightly dredge chicken in flour and shake to remove excess.

- Brown chicken in hot oil in large heavy pan over medium-high heat for 4 minutes on each side and set aside.

- Combine oregano, basil and a little salt and pepper in bowl and sprinkle mixture evenly over chicken.

- Saute onion in remaining oil in large pan, stir in wine and cook for 2 minutes.

- Return chicken to pan and add broth, potatoes, tomatoes and carrots.

- Reduce heat and simmer, stirring occasionally for 45 minutes.

- Stir in cilantro and serve over rice. Serves 8.

Wake-Up Chicken-Rice Stew

2 (12 ounce) cans white chicken meat with liquid	2 (340 g)
2 (14 ounce) cans chicken broth	2 (400 g)
1 (15 ounce) can stewed tomatoes	425 g
½ cup hot salsa	130 g
2 cups instant brown rice	370 g
1 (15 ounce) can whole kernel corn	425 g
1 (15 ounce) can cut green beans	425 g
½ teaspoon ground cumin	2 ml
½ teaspoon chili powder	2 ml

- Combine chicken, broth, stewed tomatoes, salsa and rice in heavy soup pot.

- Bring to boil, reduce heat and simmer for 10 minutes.

- Stir in corn, green beans, cumin, chili powder and a little salt and pepper.

- Bring to boil, reduce heat and cook for 5 minutes. Serves 6 to 8.

Favorite Chicken-Tomato Stew

1 pound boneless, skinless chicken breast halves, cut into strips	455 g
1 onion, chopped	
1 green bell pepper, seeded, chopped	
2 (14 ounce) cans chicken broth	2 (400 g)
2 (15 ounce) cans Mexican stewed tomatoes	2 (425 g)
2 (15 ounce) cans navy beans with liquid	2 (425 g)
1 cup salsa	265 g
2 teaspoons ground cumin	10 ml
1½ cups crushed tortilla chips	85 g

- Brown and cook chicken in stew pot on medium heat for 10 minutes.

- Add onion, bell pepper, broth, tomatoes, navy beans, salsa, cumin and a little salt and pepper.

- Bring to boil, reduce heat and simmer for 25 minutes, stirring often.

- Ladle into individual soup bowls and sprinkle crushed tortilla chips on top of stew. Serve immediately. Serves 8.

Sister's Brunswick Stew

This signature southern dish takes longer than most dishes, but it is so worth it. Cook meat one day and put stew together the next day. You'll have enough to freeze and serve for several meals. It makes an excellent one-dish meal.

1 (2 pound) boneless pork loin	910 g
3 pounds boneless, skinless chicken pieces	1.4 kg
4 medium potatoes, quartered	
3 (28 ounce) cans stewed, diced tomatoes	3 (795 g)
2 teaspoons sugar	10 ml
1 medium onion, chopped	
2 (16 ounce) packages frozen butter beans, thawed	2 (455 g)
2 (16 ounce) packages frozen corn, thawed	2 (455 g)

- Cut pork and chicken into bite-size pieces. Cover with water and cook in stew pot for 1 hour, very slowly or until tender. Skim off excess fat.

- Return meat to broth, add potatoes and cook on medium. When done, mash potatoes to thicken broth. Add tomatoes, sugar, a little salt and pepper and cook until soupy.

- Add onion and butter beans. Cook for 10 minutes on low and stir frequently.

- Add corn and cook for 5 minutes. Keep scraping bottom of pan to prevent sticking. Serves 8 to 10.

Chicken-Sausage Stew

1 (16 ounce) package frozen stew vegetables	455 g
2 (12 ounce) cans chicken breast with liquid	2 (340 g)
½ pound Italian sausage, sliced	230 g
2 (15 ounce) cans Italian stewed tomatoes	2 (425 g)
1 (14 ounce) can chicken broth	400 g
¼ teaspoon cayenne pepper	1 ml
1 cup cooked rice	165 g

- Combine all ingredients except rice and add a little salt in large heavy soup pot.

- Bring to boil, reduce heat and simmer for 25 minutes.

- Stir in cooked rice during last 5 minutes of cooking time. Serves 8.

Whipped Chicken Chowder

3 cups cooked, cubed chicken	420 g
1 (14 ounce) can chicken broth	400 g
2 (10 ounce) cans cream of potato soup	2 (280 g)
1 large onion, chopped	
3 ribs celery, sliced diagonally	
1 (16 ounce) package frozen corn, thawed	455 g
⅔ cup whipping cream	150 ml

- Combine all ingredients except cream in large soup pot with ¾ cup (175 ml) water.

- Cover and cook on low heat for about 45 minutes. Add whipping cream and heat for additional 10 minutes on low. Do not boil. Serves 6.

Chicken-Broccoli Chowder

2 (14 ounce) cans chicken broth	2 (400 g)
1 bunch fresh green onions, finely chopped, divided	
1 (10 ounce) package frozen chopped broccoli	280 g
1½ cups dry mashed potato flakes	90 g
2½ cups cooked, cut-up chicken breasts	350 g
1 (8 ounce) package shredded mozzarella cheese	230 g
1 (8 ounce) carton whipping cream	250 ml
1 cup milk	250 ml

- Combine broth, half green onions and broccoli in large saucepan. Bring to boil, reduce heat, cover and simmer for 5 minutes.

- Stir in dry potato flakes and mix until they blend well.

- Add chicken, cheese, cream, milk, 1 cup (250 ml) water and a little salt and pepper.

- Heat over medium heat and stir occasionally until hot and cheese melts, for about 5 minutes.

- Ladle into individual soup bowls and garnish with remaining chopped green onions. Serves 8.

Rich Cheddar Chowder

2 (14 ounce) cans chicken broth	2 (400 g)
4 baking potatoes, peeled, diced	
1 onion, chopped	
1 cup shredded carrots	110 g
1 green and 1 red bell pepper, seeded, chopped	
¼ cup (½ stick) butter	60 g
⅓ cup flour	40 g
1 (1 pint) carton half-and-half cream	500 ml
1½ cups milk	375 g
1 (16 ounce) package shredded sharp cheddar cheese	455 g
⅛ - ¼ teaspoon hot sauce	.5 - 1 ml

- Combine broth, potatoes, onion, carrots and bell peppers in large soup pot. Bring to a boil, reduce heat and simmer for 15 minutes.

- Melt butter in large saucepan, add flour and stir until smooth. Cook for 1 minute and stir constantly. Gradually add half-and-half cream and milk; cook over medium heat and stir constantly until mixture thickens.

- Add cheese and hot sauce to vegetable mixture and cook just until thoroughly hot; do not boil. Serves 6 to 8.

Mama Mia Chicken Chowder

2 (12 ounce) cans chicken breasts with liquid	2 (340 g)
¼ cup Italian salad dressing	60 ml
1 (15 ounce) can stewed tomatoes	425 g
1 (10 ounce) can chicken broth	280 g
2 small zucchini, chopped	
½ cup elbow macaroni	55 g
1 teaspoon dried basil	5 ml
1 cup shredded mozzarella cheese	115 g

- Combine chicken, salad dressing, tomatoes, broth, zucchini, macaroni, basil, ½ cup (125 ml) water and a little salt and pepper in large soup pot.

- Bring to boil, reduce heat and simmer for 10 minutes or until macaroni is tender.

- Serve in individual soup bowls and sprinkle cheese over each serving. Serves 4 to 6.

If you have any leftover cooked pasta, meat or vegetables, use them for instant soup ingredients. Most cooked vegetables can also be pureed and stirred in to thicken soups.

Great Northern Chili

2 onions, coarsely chopped
Olive oil
3 (15 ounce) cans
    great northern
    beans, drained   3 (425 g)
2 (14 ounce) cans
    chicken broth   2 (400 g)
2 tablespoons minced
    garlic   15 g
1 (7 ounce) can
    chopped green
    chilies   200 g
1 tablespoon ground
    cumin   15 ml
3 cups cooked, finely
    chopped chicken
    breasts   420 g
1 (8 ounce) package
    shredded Monterey
    Jack cheese   230 g

- Cook onions in a little oil in large, heavy pot for about 5 minutes, but do not brown.

- Place 1 can beans in shallow bowl and mash with fork.

- Add mashed beans, 2 remaining cans of beans, chicken broth, garlic, green chilies and cumin to soup pot. Bring to boil, reduce heat, cover and simmer for 30 minutes.

- Add chopped chicken, stir to blend well and heat until chili is thoroughly hot.

- When serving, top each bowl with 3 tablespoons (20 g) cheese. Serves 6 to 8.

White Lightning Chili

1½ cups dried navy
    beans   395 g
3 (14 ounce) cans
    chicken broth   3 (400 g)
2 tablespoons butter 30 g
1 onion, chopped
1 clove garlic,
    minced
3 cups cooked,
    chopped chicken 420 g
1½ teaspoons
    ground cumin   7 ml
½ teaspoon cayenne
    pepper   2 ml
6 (8 inch) flour
    tortillas   6 (20 cm)
Shredded Monterey
    Jack cheese

- Sort and wash beans, cover with water and soak overnight.

- Drain beans and place in soup pot and add broth, butter, 1 cup (250 ml) water, onion and garlic.

- Bring to boil, reduce heat and cover. Simmer for 2 hours and stir occasionally.

- With potato masher, mash half of beans in soup pot. Add chicken, cumin and cayenne pepper. Bring to boil, reduce heat and cover. Simmer for additional 30 minutes.

- With kitchen shears, make 4 cuts in each tortilla toward center, but not completely through center. Line serving bowls with tortillas and overlap cut edges.

- Spoon in chili and top with cheese. Serves 6 to 8.

Guess-What Chili

1 (16 ounce) package
   frozen, chopped
   onions and bell
   peppers   455 g
Olive oil
2 tablespoons minced
   garlic   15 g
2 tablespoons chili
   powder   15 g
3 teaspoons ground
   cumin   15 ml
2 pounds boneless,
   skinless chicken
   breast halves,
   cooked, cubed   910 g
2 (14 ounce) cans
   chicken broth   2 (400 g)
3 (15 ounce) cans
   pinto beans with
   jalapenos, divided 3 (425 g)

- Cook onions and bell peppers in large, heavy soup pot over medium heat with a little oil for about 5 minutes and stir occasionally.

- Add garlic, chili powder, cumin and cubed chicken and cook for additional 10 minutes.

- Stir in broth and a little salt. Bring to boil, reduce heat, cover and simmer for 15 minutes.

- Place 1 can beans in shallow bowl and mash with fork. Add mashed beans and remaining 2 cans beans to pot.

- Bring to boil, reduce heat and simmer for 10 minutes. Serves 8.

TIP: *This is delicious served with hot, buttered flour tortillas or spooned over small, original corn chips for a great one-dish meal.*

Make-Believe Chili Supper

1 pound boneless, skinless chicken breast halves, cubed	455 g
¼ cup (½ stick) butter	60 g
3 ribs celery, sliced	
2 onions, chopped	
1 red bell pepper, seeded, chopped	
2 teaspoons minced garlic	10 ml
3 (15 ounce) cans great northern beans with liquid	3 (425 g)
2 (14 ounce) cans chicken broth	2 (400g)
2 teaspoons ground cumin	10 ml
1 teaspoon dried oregano	5 ml
1 (7 ounce) can chopped green chilies	200 g
1 (8 ounce) carton sour cream	230 g

- Preheat oven to 350° (175° C).

- Sprinkle 1 teaspoon (5 ml) salt on chicken and place in sprayed 9 x 13-inch (23 x 33 cm) baking dish and bake for 15 minutes.

- Melt butter in soup pot and cook celery, onions, bell pepper and garlic on medium heat for 10 to 15 minutes.

- Stir in cooked chicken, beans, broth, cumin, oregano and green chilies and mix well.

- Bring to boil, reduce heat and simmer for 15 minutes. Stir in sour cream. Serves 8.

White Bean Chili

1 pound dried great
    northern beans   455 g
2 onions, finely
    chopped
2 ribs celery, sliced
2 tablespoons olive oil 30 ml
1 (7 ounce) can
    chopped green
    chilies   200 g
2 tablespoons minced
    garlic   15 g
1 tablespoon ground
    cumin   5 g
2 teaspoons dried
    oregano   10 ml
½ teaspoon cayenne
    pepper   2 ml
3 (14 ounce) cans
    chicken broth   3 (400 g)
1 rotisserie chicken,
    boned, cubed
1 (12 ounce) package
    shredded Monterey
    Jack cheese,
    divided   340 g

- Sort and rinse beans and place in soup pot. Cover with water 2 inches (5 cm) above beans and soak overnight. Drain beans and set aside.

- Saute onions and celery in hot oil in saucepan.

- Add green chilies, garlic, cumin, oregano and cayenne pepper, cook for 2 minutes and stir constantly.

- Transfer to soup pot and add beans, chicken broth and ½ cup (125 ml) water.

- Bring to boil and reduce heat. Cover, simmer for about 2 hours or until beans are tender; stir occasionally.

- Add chicken and 1 cup (115 g) cheese. Bring to boil, reduce heat and simmer for 10 minutes, stirring often.

- Ladle chili into individual soup bowls and top each serving with remaining cheese. Serves 8.

Cheesy Tomato Chili

1 (28 ounce) can diced tomatoes	795 g
1 (15 ounce) can kidney beans, rinsed, drained	425 g
1 (15 ounce) can pinto beans, drained	425 g
2 (14 ounce) cans chicken broth	2 (400 g)
2 (12 ounce) cans chicken breasts with liquid	2 (340 g)
1 tablespoon chili powder	15 ml
1 (8 ounce) package shredded Mexican 4-cheese blend, divided	230 g

- Combine tomatoes, kidney beans, pinto beans, broth, chicken, chili powder and a little salt and pepper in soup pot.

- Bring to boil, reduce heat and simmer for 25 minutes.

- Stir in half cheese and spoon into individual soup bowls.

- Sprinkle remaining cheese on top of each serving. Serves 8.

Corny Turkey Soup

¼ cup (½ stick) butter   60 g
1 small onion, chopped
1 red bell pepper, seeded,
    chopped
1 (3 ounce) package
    cream cheese, cubed   85 g
1 (15 ounce) can
    cream-style corn   425 g
1 (15 ounce) can whole
    kernel corn   425 g
1 (14 ounce) can chicken
    broth   400 g
½ cup milk   125 ml
2 cups cooked, cubed
    turkey   280 g
4 fresh green onions,
    sliced

- Melt butter in large, heavy soup pot, cook onion and bell pepper and stir often. Add cream cheese and cream-style corn and cook on medium heat, stir constantly until cheese melts.

- Add whole kernel corn, broth, milk and turkey, mix well and cook until soup is thoroughly hot. Sprinkle sliced green onions over top of each serving. Serves 4 to 6.

A pinch of red pepper flakes makes a wonderful addition to most soups.

Creamy Turkey Soup

3 (14 ounce) cans chicken broth	3 (400 g)
1 pound russet potatoes, peeled, cubed	455 g
3 ribs celery, sliced	
1 (15 ounce) can sliced carrots, drained	425 g
1 (10 ounce) package frozen yellow squash	280 g
2 teaspoons minced garlic	10 ml
1 teaspoon dried thyme	5 ml
1½ cups cooked, shredded turkey	210 g
1 (10 ounce) can cream of chicken soup	280 g
1 cup milk or half-and-half cream	250 ml

- Combine chicken broth, ½ cup (125 ml) water, potatoes and celery in soup pot and boil. Add a little salt and pepper and cook on medium heat for about 20 minutes or until potatoes and celery are tender. Add carrots, squash, garlic and thyme and cook for additional 10 minutes.

- Stir in shredded turkey, chicken soup and milk and heat just until soup is thoroughly hot, but do not boil. Serves 8.

Turkey with Avocado Soup

3 large potatoes,
   peeled, cubed
2 (14 ounce) cans
   chicken broth   2 (400 g)
1 teaspoon ground
   thyme   5 ml
½ pound smoked
   turkey breast,
   cubed   230 g
1 (10 ounce) package
   frozen corn   280 g
3 slices bacon, cooked
   crisp, drained
1 large avocado
4 plum tomatoes,
   coarsely chopped
1 lime

- Combine potatoes, broth and thyme in soup pot, cover and bring to boil. Reduce heat and simmer until potatoes are tender, for about 15 minutes.

- With slotted spoon transfer half of potatoes to blender or food processor, puree and pour into soup pot.

- Add turkey, remaining potatoes and corn and simmer for 5 minutes.

- Crumble bacon, peel and slice avocado.

- Add bacon, avocado, tomatoes, juice of lime and a little salt and pepper to turkey mixture. Stir gently to mix. Serves 8.

TIP: *Peel and cut avocado just before serving, because they turn dark so quickly.*

Last-Minute Turkey Help

2 (14 ounce) cans chicken broth	2 (400 g)
1 small zucchini, sliced	
1 (16 ounce) package frozen vegetable and pasta mix	455 g
1½ cups cooked, cubed turkey	210 g
4 fresh green onions, sliced	

- Combine broth, ¼ cup (60 ml) water, zucchini, vegetable mix and cubed turkey in large saucepan.

- Bring to boil, reduce heat and simmer for 10 to 12 minutes or until vegetables and pasta are tender.

- Garnish each serving with sliced green onions before serving. Serves 6.

So Easy, Creamy Turkey Soup

1 (10 ounce) can cream of celery soup	280 g
1 (10 ounce) can cream of chicken soup	280 g
1 soup can milk	
1 cup finely diced turkey	140 g

- Combine all ingredients in large saucepan. Serve hot. Serves 4.

Tasty Turkey-Veggie Soup

2 (14 ounce) cans chicken broth	2 (400 g)
2 teaspoons minced garlic	10 ml
1 (16 ounce) package frozen corn	455 g
1 (10 ounce) package frozen cut green beans	280 g
1 (10 ounce) package frozen sliced carrots	280 g
2 (15 ounce) cans stewed tomatoes	2 (425 g)
2½ cups cooked, cubed turkey	350 g
1 cup shredded mozzarella cheese	115 g

- Combine broth, 1 cup (250 ml) water, garlic, corn, green beans, carrots, tomatoes, turkey and 1 teaspoon (5 ml) salt in large, heavy soup pot.

- Bring to boil, reduce heat and simmer for 15 minutes.

- Before serving, top each bowl of soup with mozzarella cheese. Serves 8.

Hearty 15-Minute Turkey Soup

This is great served with cornbread.

1 (14 ounce) can chicken broth	400 g
3 (15 ounce) cans navy beans with liquid	3 (425 g)
1 (28 ounce) can stewed tomatoes with liquid	795 g
3 cups cooked, cubed white turkey	420 g
2 teaspoons minced garlic	10 ml
¼ teaspoon cayenne pepper	1 ml
1 (6 ounce) package baby spinach, stems removed	170 g

- Combine broth, beans, stewed tomatoes, turkey, garlic, cayenne pepper and a little salt and pepper in soup pot.

- Bring to boil, reduce heat and simmer on medium heat for about 10 minutes.

- Stir in baby spinach, bring to boil and cook, stirring constantly, for 5 minutes. Serves 8.

Turkey Tango

This is spicy, but not too spicy. It's just right! Try it with chicken too.

3 - 4 cups chopped turkey	**420 - 560 g**
2 (14 ounce) cans chicken broth	**2 (400 g)**
2 (10 ounce) cans diced tomatoes and green chilies	**2 (280 g)**
1 (15 ounce) can whole corn, drained	**425 g**
1 large onion, chopped	
1 (10 ounce) can tomato soup	**280 g**
1 teaspoon garlic powder	**5 ml**
1 teaspoon dried oregano	**5 ml**
3 tablespoons cornstarch	**25 g**

- Combine turkey, broth, tomatoes and green chilies, corn, onion, tomato soup, garlic powder and oregano in large roasting pan.

- Mix cornstarch with 3 tablespoons (45 ml) water and add to soup mixture.

- Bring mixture to a boil, reduce heat and simmer for 2 hours. Stir occasionally. Serves 6 to 8.

Smoked Turkey-Sausage Soup

2 tablespoons olive oil	30 ml
1 small onion, chopped	
1 green bell pepper, seeded, chopped	
1 (14 ounce) can chicken broth	400 g
1 medium potato, peeled, cubed	
½ teaspoon dried basil	2 ml
1 pound smoked turkey kielbasa, sliced	455 g
1 (15 ounce) can great northern beans with liquid	425 g

- Combine oil, onion and bell pepper in soup pot and cook for 5 minutes. Stir in broth, potato, basil, turkey kielbasa, 1 cup (250 ml) water and a little salt and pepper. Bring to boil, reduce heat to medium and simmer for 15 minutes or until potato is tender.

- Stir in beans and heat just until soup is thoroughly hot. Serves 6.

Fast Gobbler Fix

1 (16 ounce) package frozen chopped onions and bell peppers	455 g
Olive oil	
2 (3 ounce) packages chicken-flavored ramen noodles	2 (85 g)
2 (10 ounce) cans cream of chicken soup	2 (280 g)
1 cup cooked, cubed turkey	140 g

- Cook onions and peppers in soup pot with a little oil just until tender but not brown. Add ramen noodles with seasoning packet and 4 cups (1 L) water. Cook for 5 minutes or until noodles are tender.

- Stir in chicken soup and cubed turkey. Heat, stirring constantly, until thoroughly hot. Serves 6.

Turkey and Rice Soup

¼ cup (½ stick) butter 60 g
1 onion, chopped
3 ribs celery, finely
    chopped
1 bell pepper, seeded,
    chopped
2 (14 ounce) cans
    turkey broth   2 (400 g)
1 (6 ounce) box
    roasted-garlic
    long grain-wild
    rice   170 g
2 (10 ounce) cans
    cream of chicken
    soup   2 (280 g)
2 cups cooked, diced
    white meat turkey   480 ml
1 cup milk   250 ml

- Melt butter in soup pot over medium heat. Add onion, celery and bell pepper and cook for 10 minutes.

- Add turkey broth, 1½ cups (375 ml) water and rice and bring to boil. Reduce heat and cook on low for about 15 minutes or until rice is tender.

- Stir in chicken soup, turkey, milk and ¾ teaspoon (4 ml) pepper. Stir constantly and cook on medium heat until mixture is thoroughly hot. Serves 6.

Turkey Tenders Gobble

½ cup wild rice   95 g
3 ribs celery, sliced
1 onion, chopped
1 (4 ounce) can sliced
   mushrooms,
   drained   115 g
¼ cup (½ stick) butter   60 g
2 (14 ounce) cans
   chicken broth   2 (400 g)
1½ pounds turkey
   tenderloins   680 g
1 (15 ounce) can
   stewed tomatoes   425 g

- Mix all ingredients with ½ cup (125 ml) water in soup pot and bring to boil. Reduce heat and simmer for 45 to 55 minutes or until wild rice is tender.

- Remove turkey tenderloins with slotted spoon, cut into bite-size pieces and add to soup mixture. Heat just until thoroughly hot and serve. Serves 6.

Creole Turkey Gumbo

1 (32 ounce) carton
   chicken broth   910 g
1 pound cooked
   turkey, cubed   455 g
1 (15 ounce) can
   whole kernel corn   425 g
2 (15 ounce) cans
   stewed tomatoes   2 (425 g)
1 (10 ounce) package
   frozen chopped
   okra, thawed   280 g
¾ cup instant rice   70 g
2 teaspoons minced
   garlic   10 ml
1 teaspoon Creole
   seasoning   5 ml

- Combine all ingredients in large soup pot and bring to boil. Reduce heat and simmer for 15 minutes. Serves 8.

Turkey-Chili Supper

1 onion, finely chopped
2 (15 ounce) cans navy
    beans   2 (425 g)
2 (14 ounce) cans
    chicken broth   2 (400 g)
1 (7 ounce) can diced
    green chilies   200 g
2 teaspoons ground
    cumin   10 ml
1 teaspoon dried
    oregano   5 ml
¼ teaspoon cayenne
    pepper   1 ml
4 cups cooked, cubed
    turkey   450 g
1 (12 ounce) package
    shredded
    Monterey Jack
    cheese, divided 340 g

- Combine all ingredients except cheese in soup pot and boil. Reduce heat and simmer for 20 minutes.

- Just before serving, stir in about 2 cups (230 g) cheese and stir constantly. Ladle into individual soup bowls and sprinkle remaining cheese on top. Serves 6.

Big Bold Beefy Bowls

These beefy soups, stews and chilies are sure to please.

Big Bold Beefy Bowls Contents

Fresh Beefy Vegetable Soup

1 pound lean ground beef	455 g
1 onion, chopped	
1 (15 ounce) can Italian stewed tomatoes	425 g
1 cup freshly cut corn	165 g
1 large potato, peeled, cubed	
3 ribs celery, sliced	
1 carrot, thinly sliced	
1 (8 ounce) can green peas or lima beans	230 g
1 teaspoon dried Italian seasoning	5 ml
½ teaspoon hot sauce	2 ml
2 (14 ounce) cans beef broth	2 (400 g)
2 tablespoons flour	15 g

- Brown beef and onion in large, heavy soup pot over medium heat.

- Add stewed tomatoes, corn, potato, celery, carrot, peas, Italian seasoning, hot sauce, beef broth and 2 cups (500 ml) water. Bring to boil, reduce heat and simmer for 1 hour.

- Combine flour and ¼ cup (60 ml) water in bowl and stir to make paste.

- On medium heat, add paste to soup with a little salt and pepper and cook, stirring constantly until soup thickens. Serves 6 to 8.

Speedy Vegetable Soup

1 pound lean ground
   beef   455 g
2 (15 ounce) cans
   stewed tomatoes   2 (425 g)
3 (14 ounce) cans
   beef broth   3 (400 g)
1 (16 ounce) package
   frozen mixed
   vegetables   455 g
½ cup instant brown
   rice   95 g

- Brown ground beef in skillet, cook and stir until beef crumbles.

- Transfer to soup pot and add tomatoes, beef broth and vegetables.

- Bring to boil, reduce heat and simmer for 20 minutes, stirring occasionally.

- Add brown rice and cook on medium heat for 5 minutes. Serves 8.

Beefy Veggie Soup

1 pound lean ground beef 455 g
1 (46 ounce) can cocktail
   vegetable juice   1.4 L
1 (1 ounce) packet onion
   soup mix   30 g
1 (3 ounce) package
   beef-flavored
   ramen noodles   85 g
1 (16 ounce) package
   frozen mixed
   vegetables   455 g

- Cook beef until no longer pink in large soup pot over medium heat. Drain. Stir in cocktail juice, soup mix, seasoning packet in noodles and mixed vegetables.

- Heat mixture to boiling, reduce heat and simmer for 6 minutes or until vegetables are tender-crisp. Bring to boil again, stir in noodles and cook for 3 minutes. Serves 8.

Franks and Veggie Soup

¼ cup (½ stick) butter	60 g
2 onions, finely chopped	
1 red bell pepper, seeded, chopped	
2 teaspoons minced garlic	10 ml
1 (28 ounce) can baked beans	795 g
1 (10 ounce) package frozen mixed vegetables	280 g
1 (14 ounce) can beef broth	400 g
6 frankfurters, cut into 1-inch slices	2.5 cm
1 tablespoon Worcestershire sauce	15 ml
1 cup shredded colby cheese	115 g

- Melt butter in large saucepan over medium heat and cook onions, bell pepper and garlic for 5 minutes.

- Stir in beans, mixed vegetables, broth, frankfurters, 1 cup (250 ml) water and Worcestershire. Cook over medium heat for 5 minutes and stir occasionally.

- Ladle into individual soup bowls and sprinkle each serving with cheese. Serves 8.

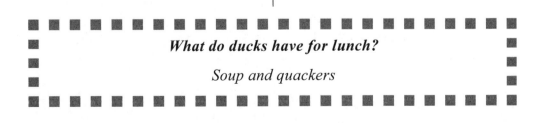

What do ducks have for lunch?

Soup and quackers

Mother's Beef-Veggie Soup

1 pound lean ground beef	455 g
1 (1 ounce) packet onion soup mix	30 g
2 (14 ounce) cans beef broth	2 (400 g)
2 (15 ounce) cans stewed tomatoes	2 (425 g)
2 (15 ounce) cans mixed vegetables with liquid	2 (425 g)
1 cup shell macaroni	105 g

- Brown beef in soup pot over high heat and drain. Reduce heat to medium and add soup mix, broth, tomatoes, mixed vegetables and 1 cup (250 ml) water and cook for 5 minutes.

- Stir in macaroni and cook on medium-high heat for 15 minutes or until macaroni is tender, stirring occasionally. Serves 8.

Vegetable-Beef Soup

1½ pounds lean ground beef	680 g
3 (15 ounce) cans mixed vegetables with liquid	3 (425 g)
1 (1 ounce) packet onion soup mix	30 g
1 (48 ounce) can cocktail vegetable juice	1.4 L
1 (14 ounce) can beef broth	400 g
½ cup barley	100 g

- Brown ground beef in roasting pan, stir to crumble and drain.

- Add all remaining ingredients with 1 cup (250 ml) water, bring to boil and simmer for 15 minutes. Serves 8.

Down-Home Beefy Soup

1½ pounds lean ground beef	680 g
1 (16 ounce) package frozen onions and peppers	455 g
2 teaspoons minced garlic	10 ml
2 (14 ounce) cans beef broth	2 (400 g)
2 (15 ounce) cans Italian stewed tomatoes	2 (425 g)
3 teaspoons Italian seasoning	15 ml
1½ cups macaroni	160 g
Shredded cheddar cheese	

- Brown and cook beef, onions and peppers, and garlic in soup pot on medium heat. Add beef broth, 2 cups (500 ml) water, stewed tomatoes and Italian seasoning and boil for 2 minutes.

- Add macaroni and cook, stirring occasionally on medium heat for about 15 minutes. When serving, sprinkle cheese over each serving. Serves 6 to 8.

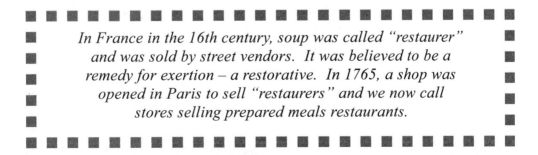

In France in the 16th century, soup was called "restaurer" and was sold by street vendors. It was believed to be a remedy for exertion – a restorative. In 1765, a shop was opened in Paris to sell "restaurers" and we now call stores selling prepared meals restaurants.

Italian Vegetable Soup

1 pound lean ground
    beef   455 g
2 teaspoons minced
    garlic   10 ml
1 green bell pepper,
    seeded, chopped
2 (14 ounce) cans beef
    broth   2 (400 g)
1 (15 ounce) can
    Italian stewed
    tomatoes   425 g
2 small zucchini,
    sliced
1 (15 ounce) can
    cannellini beans,
    rinsed, drained   425 g
1 (10 ounce) package
    frozen chopped
    spinach, thawed 280 g

- Brown and cook beef and garlic in soup pot for 5 minutes or until beef crumbles.

- Stir in bell pepper, broth, tomatoes, zucchini and beans and cook on medium heat for 15 minutes.

- Add spinach and continue cooking for additional 10 minutes. Serves 6.

Italian Beefy Veggie Soup

1 pound lean ground beef	455 g
2 teaspoons minced garlic	10 ml
2 (15 ounce) cans Italian stewed tomatoes	2 (425 g)
2 (14 ounce) cans beef broth	2 (400 g)
2 teaspoons Italian seasoning	10 ml
1 (16 ounce) package frozen mixed vegetables	455 g
⅓ cup shell macaroni	35 g
1 (8 ounce) package shredded Italian cheese	230 g

- Cook beef and garlic in large soup pot for 5 minutes.

- Stir in tomatoes, broth, 1 cup (250 ml) water, seasoning, mixed vegetables, macaroni and a little salt and pepper.

- Bring to boil, reduce heat and simmer for 10 to 15 minutes or until macaroni is tender.

- Ladle into individual serving bowls and sprinkle several tablespoons cheese over top of soup. Serves 8.

Almost all soups can be made in advance. Many, in fact, are better on the second or third day, after the flavors have blended.

No-Brainer Heidelberg Soup

2 (10 ounce) cans
   potato soup   2 (280 g)
1 (10 ounce) can
   cream of celery
   soup   280 g
1 soup can milk
6 slices salami,
   chopped
10 green onions,
   chopped

- Cook potato soup, celery soup and milk in large saucepan on medium heat, stirring constantly, just until thoroughly hot.

- Saute salami and onions in sprayed skillet and add to soup.

- Heat thoroughly and serve hot. Serves 6.

Easy Mexican Beef Soup

2 pounds lean ground
   beef   910 g
2 (15 ounce) cans chili
   without beans   2 (425 g)
3 (14 ounce) cans beef
   broth   3 (400 g)
2 (15 ounce) cans
   Mexican stewed
   tomatoes   2 (425 g)
2 (4 ounce) cans
   diced green chilies 2 (115 g)

- Brown ground beef until no longer pink in skillet and transfer to soup pot.

- Add chili, broth, stewed tomatoes, green chilies, 1 cup (250 ml) water, 1 teaspoon (5 ml) salt and stir well.

- Cover and cook on medium-low heat for about 45 minutes. Serves 8.

Southwestern Soup

1½ pounds lean ground beef	680 g
1 large onion, chopped	
2 (15 ounce) cans pinto beans with liquid	2 (425 g)
1 (15 ounce) can ranch-style beans, drained	425 g
2 (15 ounce) cans whole kernel corn with liquid	2 (425 g)
2 (15 ounce) cans Mexican stewed tomatoes	2 (425 g)
2 (1 ounce) packets taco seasoning	2 (30 g)

- Brown beef and onion in large soup pot, stir until beef crumbles and drain.

- Add beans, corn, tomatoes and 1½ cups (375 ml) water.

- Bring to boil, reduce heat and stir in taco seasoning. Simmer for 25 minutes. Serves 8.

Kitchen-Sink Taco Soup

1¼ pounds lean ground beef	570 g
1 onion, chopped	
1 (0.4 ounce) packet ranch dressing mix	10 g
2 (15 ounce) cans pinto beans with liquid	2 (425 g)
1 (15 ounce) can whole kernel corn with liquid	425 g
1 (15 ounce) can cream-style corn	425 g
3 (15 ounce) cans Mexican stewed tomatoes with liquid	3 (425 g)
Tortilla chips	
1 (8 ounce) package shredded Monterey Jack cheese	230 g

- Brown ground beef and onion in skillet, drain and stir in ranch dressing mix.

- Combine beef-onion mixture, beans, corn, cream-style corn and stewed tomatoes in roasting pan.

- Bring to boil, lower heat and simmer for 10 to 15 minutes.

- Serve over tortilla chips and sprinkle with cheese. Serves 6.

Cantina Taco Soup

1½ pounds lean ground
    beef   **680 g**
1 (1 ounce) packet
    taco seasoning   **30 g**
2 (15 ounce) cans
    Mexican stewed
    tomatoes   **2 (425 g)**
1 (15 ounce) can
    whole kernel
    corn, drained   **425 g**
Crushed tortilla chips
Shredded cheddar cheese

- Brown ground beef in skillet until it is no longer pink and transfer to soup pot.

- Add taco seasoning, tomatoes, corn and 1 cup (250 ml) water.

- On high heat, bring to boil, reduce heat and simmer for about 35 minutes.

- When serving, spoon 1 heaping tablespoon (15 ml) crushed tortilla chips and 1 heaping tablespoon (10 g) cheese over each serving. Serves 4 to 6.

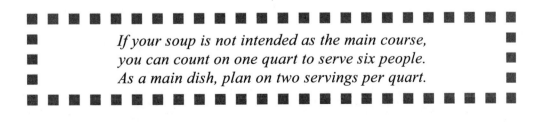

If your soup is not intended as the main course,
you can count on one quart to serve six people.
As a main dish, plan on two servings per quart.

Across-the-Border Tamale Soup

1 pound lean ground beef	455 g
1 (16 ounce) package frozen chopped onions and bell peppers	455 g
2 tablespoons olive oil	30 ml
1 (10 ounce) package frozen corn	280 g
2 (14 ounce) cans beef broth	2 (400 g)
1 (15 ounce) can pinto beans with liquid	425 g
2 tablespoons chili powder	30 ml
1 teaspoon ground cumin	5 ml
1 (28 ounce) can tamales with liquid, unwrapped, quartered	795 g

- Brown beef, onions and bell peppers in oil in large skillet.

- Transfer to soup pot and add corn, broth, beans, chili powder, cumin and a little salt and pepper.

- Bring to boil, reduce heat and simmer for 30 minutes. About 15 minutes prior to serving, add tamale chunks and heat thoroughly. Stir gently so tamales will not break. Serve hot. Serves 8.

TIP: For a spicier soup, you could add 1 (10 ounce/280 g) can tomatoes and green chilies.

Albondigas Soup

This is a very traditional meatball-potato soup.

2 pounds lean ground
   beef   910 g
1 cup breadcrumbs   60 g
1 onion, chopped
2 eggs
2 teaspoons ground cumin 10 ml
2 cloves garlic, minced
¼ cup bacon drippings
   or butter   55 g
2 tablespoons flour   15 g
3 tablespoons snipped
   cilantro   20 g
2 large potatoes, peeled,
   cubed

- Combine beef, breadcrumbs, onion, eggs, cumin and garlic with 1 teaspoon (5 ml) salt and ½ teaspoon (2 ml) pepper in bowl. Mix well and form into meatballs about 1¼ inches (2.5 cm) in diameter.

- Brown meatballs on all sides in large skillet. Transfer to bowl and set aside.

- Heat bacon drippings or butter in same skillet and sprinkle flour on top. Stir constantly until flour browns. (Do not burn.)

- Add 4 cups (1 L) hot water, cilantro and ½ teaspoon (2 ml) salt and continue to stir until liquid boils.

- Add potatoes and meatballs and simmer until potatoes are done. Serves 6.

Quick Enchilada Soup

1 pound lean ground
  beef, browned,
  drained   455 g
1 (15 ounce) can
  Mexican stewed
  tomatoes   425 g
2 (15 ounce) cans
  pinto beans with
  liquid   2 (425 g)
1 (15 ounce) can
  whole kernel corn
  with liquid   425 g
1 onion, chopped
2 (10 ounce) cans
  enchilada sauce   2 (280 g)
1 (8 ounce) package
  shredded 4-cheese
  blend   230 g

- Combine beef, tomatoes, beans, corn, onion, enchilada sauce and 1 cup (250 ml) water in soup pot.

- Bring to boil, reduce heat and simmer for 35 minutes.

- When serving, sprinkle a little shredded cheese over each serving. Serves 6.

Easy Meaty Minestrone

2 (26 ounce) cans
  minestrone soup   2 (740 g)
1 (15 ounce) can pinto
  beans with liquid   425 g
1 (18 ounce) package
  frozen Italian
  meatballs, thawed   510 g
1 (5 ounce) package
  grated parmesan
  cheese   145 g

- Combine soups, beans, meatballs and ½ cup (125 ml) water in large saucepan.

- Bring to boil, reduce heat and simmer for about 15 minutes.

- To serve, sprinkle each serving with parmesan cheese. Serves 6.

Spaghetti Soup

1 (7 ounce) package
precut spaghetti   200 g
1 (18 ounce) package
frozen, cooked
meatballs, thawed   510 g
1 (28 ounce) jar spaghetti
sauce   795 g
1 (15 ounce) can Mexican
stewed tomatoes   425 g

- Cook spaghetti in soup pot with 2 quarts (2 L) boiling water and a little salt for about 6 minutes (no need to drain).

- When spaghetti is done, add meatballs, spaghetti sauce and stewed tomatoes and cook until mixture heats through. Serves 8.

TIP: If you want to garnish each soup bowl, sprinkle with 2 tablespoons (15 g) shredded mozzarella cheese or whatever cheese you have in the refrigerator.

Quick Beef-Veggie Soup

1 pound round steak,
cubed   455 g
2 (14 ounce) cans
beef broth   2 (400 g)
1 (6 ounce) can
tomato sauce   170 g
1 (15 ounce) can
Mexican stewed
tomatoes   425 g
1 (15 ounce) can
mixed vegetables
with liquid   425 g
1 (8 ounce) can whole
kernel corn,
drained   230 g

- Brown steak on medium heat in soup pot for 10 minutes. Add beef broth and tomato sauce and simmer for 15 minutes.

- Stir in stewed tomatoes, mixed vegetables and corn and cook for additional 10 minutes. Serves 6.

Chunky Beefy Noodle Soup

1 pound beef round steak, cubed	455 g
1 onion, chopped	
2 ribs celery, sliced	
1 tablespoon oil	15 ml
1 tablespoon chili powder	15 ml
½ teaspoon dried oregano	2 ml
1 (15 ounce) can stewed tomatoes	425 g
2 (14 ounce) cans beef broth	2 (400 g)
½ (8 ounce) package egg noodles	½ (230 g)
1 green bell pepper, seeded, chopped	

- Cook and stir cubed steak, onion and celery in soup pot with oil for 15 minutes or until beef browns.

- Stir in 2 cups (500 ml) water, 1 teaspoon (5 ml) salt, chili powder, oregano, stewed tomatoes and beef broth.

- Bring to boil, reduce heat and simmer for 1 hour 30 minutes to 2 hours or until beef is tender.

- Stir in noodles and bell pepper and heat to boiling.

- Reduce heat and simmer for 10 to 15 minutes or until noodles are tender. Serves 6.

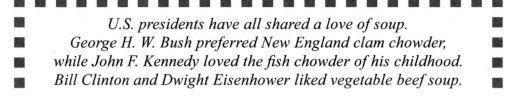

U.S. presidents have all shared a love of soup.
George H. W. Bush preferred New England clam chowder,
while John F. Kennedy loved the fish chowder of his childhood.
Bill Clinton and Dwight Eisenhower liked vegetable beef soup.

Meatball Soup

1 (18 ounce) package
    frozen, cooked
    Italian meatballs   510 g
2 (14 ounce) cans
    beef broth   2 (400 g)
2 (15 ounce) cans
    Italian stewed
    tomatoes   2 (425 g)
1 (16 ounce) package
    frozen stew
    vegetables   455 g

- Place meatballs, beef broth
  and stewed tomatoes in
  large saucepan.

- Bring to boil, reduce heat and
  simmer for 10 minutes or until
  meatballs are thoroughly hot.

- Add vegetables and cook on
  medium heat for 10 minutes.
  Serves 6 to 8.

TIP: If you like your soup thicker,
    mix 2 tablespoons (15 g)
    cornstarch in ¼ cup (60 ml)
    water and stir into soup,
    bring to boiling and stir
    constantly until soup thickens.

Steak Soup

1 pound ground
    sirloin steak   455 g
2 (10 ounce) cans
    vegetable soup   2 (280 g)
2 (10 ounce) cans
    tomatoes and
    green chilies
    with liquid   2 (280 g)

- Brown ground sirloin in large
  skillet, crumble and drain.

- Stir in soups, tomatoes and
  green chilies.

- Heat on medium-low for
  15 to 20 minutes or until hot.
  Stir often. Serves 4.

Black Bean-Barbecue Soup

1 onion, finely
   chopped
2 tablespoons olive oil   30 ml
2 teaspoons minced
   garlic   10 ml
2 (14 ounce) cans
   chicken broth   2 (400 g)
3 (15 ounce) cans
   black beans,
   rinsed, drained   3 (425 g)
1 (10 ounce) can
   diced tomatoes
   and green chilies   280 g
1 pound shredded
   barbecue beef   455 g
2 tablespoons red
   wine vinegar   30 ml
Shredded Monterey
   Jack cheese

- Saute onion in oil in soup pot over medium heat, stir in garlic and saute 1 more minute.

- Stir in broth, beans and tomatoes and green chilies. Reduce heat and simmer, stirring often for 15 minutes.

- Process 1 cup (250 ml) bean mixture in food processor until smooth.

- Return puree to soup pot, add beef and simmer for 10 minutes.

- Stir in vinegar and garnish each bowl with cheese. Serves 6 to 8.

Savory soups and stews often taste better if made a day or two in advance and reheated just before serving.

Menudo

*This could also be called
Mexican Hangover Helper
or at least it is reported to be a
sure cure for the morning after.*

2 pounds tripe	**910 g**
1 bunch green onions with tops, chopped	
3 cloves garlic, minced	
¾ cup snipped fresh cilantro leaves, divided	**10 g**
Fresh lime slices	

- Wash tripe very well and dry with paper towels. Place tripe in soup pot with enough water to cover plus 3 inches (8 cm).

- Add onions and garlic, bring to boil, reduce heat and simmer for 6 to 8 hours until tripe is tender. Add water if necessary.

- When tripe is tender, remove from pot and cool for about 15 minutes. Cut into small pieces and return to soup pot.

- Add ¼ cup (5 g) cilantro and cook for an additional 1 to 2 hours. Serve in large soup bowls and garnish with cilantro and lime slices. Serves 4.

TIP: Menudo or tripe soup is a favorite in Mexico. Tripe is the inner lining of beef stomach, is very tough and requires long cooking times.

Blue Norther Stew

Cold fronts in the south are called
northers. This is a great choice for
one of those cold, winter days.

1½ pounds lean ground beef	**680 g**
1 onion, chopped	
1 (0.4 ounce) packet taco seasoning	**10 g**
1 (0.4 ounce) packet ranch dressing mix	**10 g**
1 (15 ounce) can whole kernel corn, drained	**425 g**
1 (15 ounce) can kidney beans with liquid	**425 g**
2 (15 ounce) cans pinto beans	**2 (425 g)**
2 (15 ounce) cans Mexican stewed tomatoes	**2 (425 g)**
1 (10 ounce) can tomatoes and green chilies	**280 g**

- Brown ground beef and onion in large roasting pan.

- Add both packets seasonings and mix well.

- Add corn, beans, stewed tomatoes, tomatoes and green chilies, and 1 cup (250 ml) water, mix well and simmer for about 30 minutes. Serves 8.

Bronco Stew

Hang on for this hot ride!

2 pounds ground round beef	**910 g**
Olive oil	
1 (16 ounce) package frozen, chopped onions and bell peppers	**455 g**
1 (14 ounce) can beef broth	**400 g**
1 (1 ounce) packet taco seasoning	**30 g**
2 (15 ounce) cans Mexican stewed tomatoes	**2 (425 g)**
2 (15 ounce) cans pinto beans with jalapenos	**2 (425 g)**
1 (16 ounce) package cubed Velveeta® cheese	**455 g**
1 (13 ounce) package tortilla chips, crushed	**370 g**

- Brown beef on all sides in a little oil in stew pot on high heat and stir often.

- Add onion and bell peppers, and cook for 3 minutes.

- Add broth and taco seasoning, reduce heat and simmer for 35 to 45 minutes or until most of liquid evaporates.

- Stir in tomatoes and beans and heat just until mixture is thoroughly hot. Add cheese and stir until cheese melts.

- Place about ¾ cup (40 g) crushed chips in bottom of individual soup bowls, spoon stew over chips and serve immediately. Serves 8.

Vegetable-Beef Stew

1 pound stew meat	455 g
1 (14 ounce) can beef broth	400 g
1 (28 ounce) can stewed tomatoes	795 g
2 (15 ounce) cans mixed vegetables with liquid	2 (425 g)
½ cup barley	100 g

- Combine meat, broth and 2 cups (250 ml) water and a little salt and pepper in large stew pot and bring to boil.

- Reduce heat to low and cook for 1 hour.

- Stir in all remaining ingredients and cook on medium heat for 30 minutes. Serves 6.

Minute Stew

1 pound extra-lean ground beef	455 g
1 (14 ounce) can beef broth	400 g
1 (15 ounce) can stewed tomatoes with onions	425 g
1 (8 ounce) can whole kernel corn, drained	230 g
1 (15 ounce) can mixed vegetables	425 g

- Brown ground meat in skillet and drain.

- Add broth, tomatoes, corn and vegetables to skillet and mix well.

- Simmer for 20 to 30 minutes and stir often. Serves 6.

Quick Brunswick Stew

Brunswick Stew is a favorite in Virginia and other southern states. The original version takes all day to make, but this is a quick substitute that is great in a pinch.

1 (15 ounce) can beef stew	425 g
1 (15 ounce) can chicken stew	425 g
1 (15 ounce) can lima beans with liquid	425 g
2 (15 ounce) cans stewed tomatoes with liquid	2 (425 g)
1 (15 ounce) can whole kernel corn	425 g
½ teaspoon hot sauce	2 ml

- Combine beef stew, chicken stew, beans, tomatoes and corn in large stew pot on medium heat. Bring to a boil, reduce heat and simmer for 20 minutes.

- Brunswick Stew needs to be a little spicy, so stir in ¼ teaspoon (1 ml) hot sauce at first, taste and add more if needed. If you don't want spicy, add 1 tablespoon (15 ml) Worcestershire sauce to stew. It is best served with hot cornbread muffins. Serves 6.

Fresh chopped parsley added in the last few minutes of cooking adds a wonderful fresh flavor to soups and stews.

Baked Pinto Bean Stew

1 cup dried pinto beans	125 g
1 pound beef stew meat	455 g
1 onion, chopped	
1 (6 ounce) can tomato paste	230 g
¼ cup packed brown sugar	55 g
½ teaspoon dry mustard	2 ml
¼ teaspoon ground cinnamon	1 ml

- Preheat oven to 325° (160° C).

- Place beans in large, heavy pot, add 5 cups (1.2 L) water and boil for 2 minutes.

- Add remaining ingredients with a little salt and pepper. Cover and bake for 2 hours.

- Remove from oven and stir mixture well. Return to oven, cover and bake for additional 3 hours or until beans and beef are tender. Serves 6.

Stroganoff Stew

1 (1 ounce) packet onion soup mix	30 g
2 (10 ounce) cans golden mushroom soup	2 (280 g)
2 pounds stew meat	910 g
1 (8 ounce) carton sour cream	230 g
Noodles, cooked	

- Preheat oven to 275° (140° C).

- Combine soup mix, mushroom soup and 2 soup cans water and pour over stew meat in roasting pan.

- Cover tightly and bake for 6 to 8 hours.

- When ready to serve, stir in sour cream, return mixture to oven until it heats thoroughly and serve over noodles. Serves 6.

Meat and Potato Stew

2 pounds beef stew meat	910 g
2 (15 ounce) cans new potatoes, drained	2 (425 g)
1 (15 ounce) can sliced carrots, drained	425 g
2 (10 ounce) cans French onion soup	2 (280 g)

- Season meat with a little salt and pepper and cook with 2 cups (500 ml) water in large pot for 1 hour.

- Add potatoes, carrots and onion soup and mix well.

- Bring to boil, reduce heat and simmer for 30 minutes. Serves 6.

Oven-Baked Beef Stew

1 tablespoon flour	10 g
¾ pound beef chuck, cubed	340 g
¾ cup chopped onion	120 g
¼ teaspoon basil	1 ml
2 potatoes, peeled, cubed	
2 carrots, peeled, sliced	
¼ cup dry red wine	60 ml
1 (10 ounce) can tomato soup	280 g

- Preheat oven to 325° (160° C).

- Combine flour with a little salt and pepper and pat onto both sides of meat. Brown meat in large iron skillet. Transfer to large deep skillet.

- Add all remaining ingredients with 1¼ cups (310 ml) water; cover and bake for about 1 hour. Serves 4 to 6.

Pirate Stew for the Crew

If you can open cans, you can make this stew. Don't let the number of ingredients get to you. Leave something out if you get tired of opening cans, but by all means, you can handle this recipe.

3 pounds beef chuck roast, cubed	1.4 kg
Olive oil	
2 (15 ounce) cans diced tomatoes	2 (425 g)
2 (32 ounce) cans V8® juice	2 (950 ml)
2 (15 ounce) cans green beans, drained	2 (425 g)
2 (15 ounce) cans field peas with snaps, drained	2 (425 g)
2 (15 ounce) cans green peas, drained	2 (425 g)
2 (14 ounce) cans cut okra, drained	2 (400 g)
2 (16 ounce) packages frozen lima beans	2 (455 g)
2 (16 ounce) packages frozen yellow corn	2 (455 g)
1 (16 ounce) package frozen white corn	455 g
2 pounds onion, peeled, diced	910 g
4 pounds potatoes, peeled, cubed	2 kg
1 teaspoon dried rosemary	5 ml

- Brown roast in oil in large stew pot. Add remaining ingredients with 1-quart (1 L) water and a little salt and pepper.

- Simmer all day. Remove excess fat before serving. Serves 12 to 16.

TIP: This recipe makes enough for several meals so freeze some for later.

Blue Ribbon Beef Stew

1 (2½ pound) boneless beef chuck roast, cubed	1.2 kg
⅓ cup flour	40 g
2 (14 ounce) cans beef broth	2 (400 g)
1 teaspoon dried thyme	5 ml
2 teaspoons minced garlic	10 ml
1 pound new (red) potatoes with peel, sliced	455 g
2 large carrots, sliced	
3 ribs celery, sliced	
2 onions, finely chopped	
1 (10 ounce) package frozen green peas	280 g

- Dredge beef in flour and 1 teaspoon (5 ml) salt; reserve leftover flour. Brown half beef in stew pot over medium heat for about 10 minutes and transfer to plate.

- Repeat with remaining beef. Add reserved flour to stew pot and cook, stirring constantly, for 1 minute.

- Stir in beef broth, ½ cup (125 ml) water, thyme and garlic and bring to boil. Reduce heat, simmer for 50 minutes and stir occasionally.

- Add potatoes, carrots, celery and onion and cook for 30 minutes.

- Stir in green peas, a little salt and pepper; heat to boiling. Serve hot. Serves 6.

Border-Crossing Stew

1½ pounds round steak, cubed	680 g
2 onions, chopped	
1 (14 ounce) can beef broth	400 g
1 (15 ounce) can Mexican stewed tomatoes	425 g
1 (7 ounce) can chopped green chilies	200 g
3 baking potatoes, peeled, cubed	
2 teaspoons minced garlic	10 ml
2 teaspoons ground cumin	10 ml

- Brown cubed steak and onion in stew pot, cook for 10 minutes and stir often.

- Mix in beef broth, tomatoes, green chilies, potatoes, garlic, cumin, 1 cup (250 ml) water and a little salt and pepper.

- Cover and cook on medium-low heat for 35 minutes or until potatoes are tender. Serves 6.

Steakhouse Stew

1 pound boneless beef sirloin steak, cubed	455 g
Olive oil	
1 (15 ounce) can stewed tomatoes	425 g
1 (10 ounce) can French onion soup	280 g
1 (10 ounce) can tomato soup	280 g
1 (16 ounce) package frozen stew vegetables, thawed	455 g

- Cook steak in skillet with a little oil until juices evaporate. Transfer to stew pot or roasting pan.

- Add 1 cup (250 ml) water, tomatoes, soups and vegetables and heat to boiling. Reduce heat to low and simmer for 35 minutes. Serves 6.

Green Chile Stew Pot (Caldillo)

Caldillo or stew is a traditional Mexican dish served on special occasions.

2 pounds round steak, cubed   **910 g**
Canola oil
2 onions, chopped
2 potatoes, peeled, diced
2 cloves garlic, minced
6 - 8 fresh green chilies, roasted, peeled, seeded, diced

- Sprinkle round steak with 1 tablespoon (15 ml) salt; heat oil in large skillet and brown meat. Put onions, potatoes and garlic in same skillet and cook until onions are translucent.

- Pour all ingredients from skillet into large stew pot. Add chilies, 1 teaspoon (5 ml) salt and ½ teaspoon (2 ml) pepper and enough water to cover.

- Bring to boil, lower heat and simmer for 1 to 2 hours or until meat and potatoes are tender. Serves 6.

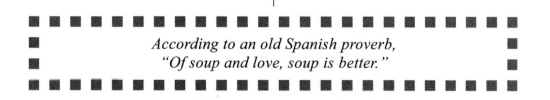

According to an old Spanish proverb,
"Of soup and love, soup is better."

Cattle Drive Chili Stew

3 pounds stew meat   1.4 kg
3 tablespoons olive oil 45 ml
1 medium onion,
    chopped
3 ribs celery, chopped
2 (15 ounce) cans
    Mexican stewed
    tomatoes with
    liquid   2 (425 g)
2 (14 ounce) cans
    beef broth   2 (400 g)
1 (10 ounce) package
    frozen whole
    kernel corn   280 g
1 cup diced, fresh
    green chilies   240 g

- Brown stew meat on all sides in large skillet with oil and transfer to large stew pot.

- Saute onion and celery in skillet drippings until translucent and pour drippings and vegetables into stew pot.

- Stir in tomatoes, beef broth, corn, chilies, 2 teaspoons (10 ml) salt and ¼ teaspoon (1 ml) pepper and bring to boil.

- Reduce heat and simmer for 2 hours or until stew meat is tender. Serves 8.

TIP: If soup is too thin, add ¼ cup (15 g) instant mashed potato flakes.

Did you know that lettuce loves fat? Fat can be removed from hot soup by floating a large lettuce leaf on the surface.

Chili-Soup Warmer

1 (10 ounce) can
    tomato bisque soup   280 g
1 (10 ounce) can fiesta
    chili-beef soup   280 g
1 (10 ounce) can chili   280 g
1 (14 ounce) can beef
    broth   400 g
Crackers

- Combine soups, chili and broth in saucepan. Add amount of water to produce desired thickness of soup.

- Heat and serve hot with crackers. Serves 4 to 6.

Easy Chunky Chili

2 pounds premium-cut
    stew meat   910 g
1 (10 ounce) can beef
    broth   280 g
1 onion, chopped
2 (15 ounce) cans
    diced tomatoes   2 (425 g)
1 (10 ounce) can
    tomatoes and
    green chilies   280 g
2 (15 ounce) cans
    pinto beans with
    liquid   2 (425 g)
1½ tablespoons chili
    powder   10 g
2 teaspoons ground
    cumin   10 ml
1 teaspoon oregano   5 ml

- If stew meat is in fairly large chunks, cut each chunk in half. Brown stew meat in large skillet and add all remaining ingredients.

- Bring to boil, reduce heat and cook on low for 1 hour. Serves 6.

Cadillac Chili

1½ pounds lean ground beef	680 g
2 pounds chili ground beef	910 g
1 onion, chopped	
Olive oil	
1 (15 ounce) can tomato sauce	425 g
1 (10 ounce) can diced tomatoes and green chilies	280 g
4 tablespoons ground cumin	25 g
1 teaspoon oregano	5 ml
2 tablespoons chili powder	15 g
1 (15 ounce) can pinto beans with liquid	425 g

- Combine meats and onion in a little oil in large roasting pan and brown.

- Add tomato sauce, tomatoes and green chilies, cumin, oregano, chili powder, 2 cups (500 ml) water and a little salt.

- Bring to a boil, reduce heat and simmer for 2 hours.

- Add beans and heat until thoroughly hot. Serves 6.

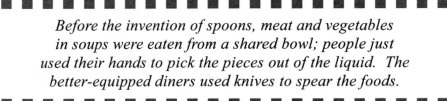

Before the invention of spoons, meat and vegetables in soups were eaten from a shared bowl; people just used their hands to pick the pieces out of the liquid. The better-equipped diners used knives to spear the foods.

Beefy Bean Chili

2 pounds lean ground beef	910 g
3 ribs celery, sliced	
1 onion, chopped	
1 bell pepper, seeded, chopped	
2 teaspoons minced garlic	10 ml
1 (15 ounce) can tomato sauce	425 g
3 tablespoons chili powder	30 g
2 (15 ounce) cans pinto beans with liquid	2 (425 g)
1 - 2 cups crushed tortilla chips	55 - 110 g

- Brown and cook ground beef in large soup pot over medium heat until meat crumbles.

- Add celery, onion, bell pepper and minced garlic. Cook for 5 minutes or until vegetables are tender, but not brown.

- Stir in tomato sauce, chili powder, 2 cups (500 ml) water and a little salt and pepper and mix well.

- Bring mixture to a boil, reduce heat and simmer for 35 minutes.

- Add beans during last 15 minutes of cooking time.

- Ladle into individual serving bowls and top each serving with several tablespoons crushed tortilla chips. Serves 6.

Baked Chili

1½ cups dried pinto beans	185 g
1½ pounds beef round steak, cubed	680 g
3 onions, finely chopped	
3 teaspoons minced garlic	15 ml
3 (8 ounce) cans tomato sauce	3 (230 g)
3 tablespoons chili powder	30 g
1 tablespoon ground cumin	15 ml
½ teaspoon cayenne pepper	2 ml
1 (8 ounce) package shredded Mexican 4-cheese blend	230 g

- Preheat oven to 325° (160° C).

- Heat beans and 6 cups (1.4 L) water to boiling in large, heavy pot and boil for 2 minutes.

- Stir in all remaining ingredients except cheese, cover and bake for about 3 hours.

- Remove from oven and stir well. Return to oven and bake for additional 1 hour.

- Garnish each individual bowl with cheese. Serves 6 to 8.

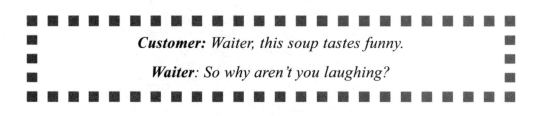

Customer: Waiter, this soup tastes funny.

Waiter: So why aren't you laughing?

Hearty Beef Chili

3 tablespoons olive oil,
    divided   **45 ml**
2 pounds round steak,
    cubed   **910 g**
2 onions, chopped
4 cloves garlic,
    minced
¼ cup tomato paste   **65 g**
2 - 4 canned jalapeno
    peppers, stemmed,
    seeded, minced
3 tablespoons chili
    powder   **30 g**
1 teaspoon oregano   **5 ml**
1 teaspoon ground
    cumin   **5 ml**
2 (15 ounce) cans
    diced tomatoes
    with liquid   **2 (425 g)**
1 (10 ounce) can
    beef broth   **280 g**
1 (7 ounce) can
    chopped green
    chilies   **200 g**
1 (15 ounce) can pinto
    beans, drained   **425 g**

- Heat 1 tablespoon (15 ml) oil in soup pot and brown beef. Transfer meat to bowl and set aside.

- Heat remaining 2 tablespoons (30 ml) oil in soup pot and add onion and garlic. Cook for about 3 minutes, stir in tomato paste, jalapenos, chili powder, 1 teaspoon (5 ml) each of salt and pepper, oregano and cumin.

- Add tomatoes, meat, beef broth, 1 cup (250 ml) water and green chilies.

- Bring to boil, reduce heat and simmer for 2 hours or until meat is tender and chili thickens.

- Stir in beans and continue simmering for about 20 minutes. Serves 6.

TIP: If you like it extra hot, leave the seeds and veins in the jalapenos. If you take the seeds out, rubber gloves will protect your hands from the juices.

Chile, New Mexico-Style

This New Mexico chile is also called "Chili Con Carne".

Canola oil
2 pounds chuck or
   pork roast, cubed   910 g
2 (14 ounce) cans
   beef broth   2 (400 g)
6 - 8 dried New
   Mexico red chilies,
   ground or
   4 - 5 dried chipotle
   chilies, ground
4 - 6 cloves garlic,
   minced
3 tablespoons paprika 30 g
1 teaspoon ground
   cumin   5 ml
1 tablespoon oregano 15 ml

- Heat oil in large skillet or large, heavy pot and brown meat on all sides.

- Add beef broth and ground chilies and bring to a boil. Reduce heat, simmer for about 2 hours and stir occasionally.

- Add garlic, paprika, cumin, oregano and 1 teaspoon (5 ml) salt.

- Cover and simmer for 15 minutes. Stir occasionally and skim grease. Serves 6.

Taco Chili

2 pounds very lean stew meat	910 g
1 (14 ounce) can beef broth	400 g
2 (15 ounce) cans Mexican stewed tomatoes	2 (425 g)
1 (1 ounce) packet taco seasoning mix	30 g
2 (15 ounce) cans pinto beans with liquid	2 (425 g)
1 (15 ounce) can whole kernel corn with liquid	425 g
1 (8 ounce) package shredded Mexican 4-cheese blend	230 g

- Cut large pieces of stew meat in half and brown in large skillet.

- Combine stew meat, broth, tomatoes, taco seasoning mix, beans, corn and ¾ cup (175 ml) water in stew pot. (If you are not into "spicy", use original recipe stewed tomatoes instead of Mexican.)

- Bring to boil, reduce heat and simmer for 1 hour or until meat is tender. Sprinkle in cheese on top of each serving. Serves 8.

TIP: For garnish top each serving with chopped green onions.

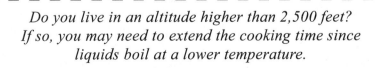

Do you live in an altitude higher than 2,500 feet?
If so, you may need to extend the cooking time since
liquids boil at a lower temperature.

Ancho-Spiked Chili

5 ancho chilies
2 tablespoons olive oil   **30 ml**
2 onions, chopped
2 cloves garlic, minced
1 pound lean boneless
**   beef, cubed**   **455 g**
1 pound lean boneless
**   pork, cubed**   **455 g**
1 fresh or canned
**   jalapeno pepper,**
**   seeded, minced**
1 teaspoon dried,
**   crushed oregano**   **5 ml**
1 teaspoon ground
**   cumin**   **5 ml**
½ cup dry red wine   **125 ml**

- Rinse ancho chilies, remove stems, seeds and veins and place in saucepan with 2 cups (500 ml) water. Bring to boil, turn off heat and let stand, covered for 30 minutes or until chilies soften.

- Pour chilies with liquid into blender and process until smooth.

- Heat oil in soup pot and saute onion, garlic and meats until meat is light brown. Add jalapeno pepper, 1 teaspoon (5 ml) salt, oregano, cumin, wine and ancho puree.

- Bring to boil, reduce heat, cover and simmer for 2 hours.

- Uncover and simmer for about 30 minutes or until chili thickens slightly. Serves 6.

Chile Verde con Carne

"Chile con carne" means chili with meat. Verde refers to the fresh green chilies.

2 - 3 pounds sirloin or tenderloin, cubed	**910 g - 1.4 kg**
½ cup (1 stick) butter	**115 g**
2 onions, chopped	
4 - 6 cloves garlic, minced	
8 - 10 fresh whole green chilies, peeled, seeded, chopped	
1 tablespoon ground cumin	**15 ml**
2 teaspoons oregano	**10 ml**

- Brown sirloin in butter in large skillet. Reduce heat to low and add all remaining ingredients plus 1 cup (250 ml) water and, 1 teaspoon (5 ml) each of salt and pepper. Cover and simmer for about 2 to 3 hours.

- Stir occasionally and add ½ to 1 cup (125 to 250 ml) water if necessary. Remove cover, taste for flavor and adjust seasonings, if needed. Serves 6.

TIP: To save time, chili powder may be used instead of roasting fresh green chilies, but the flavor of fresh chilies is the secret to the best chili.

A Bowl of Red

Proper name for Real Texas Chili, make no beans about it. At the first Original Terlingua International Cook-Off in Terlingua, Texas in 1966, Frank X. Tolbert and Wick Fowler called real Texas chili the name, "Bowl of Red".

½ cup beef suet or canola oil	125 ml
3 pounds sirloin steak, cubed	1.4 kg
6 - 8 dried chile colorado peppers, ground or 4 - 5 dried chipotle chile peppers, ground	
1 - 2 whole jalapeno peppers, divided	
4 - 6 cloves garlic, minced	
½ cup paprika	50 g
2 tablespoons ground cumin	15 g
2 tablespoons masa harina, optional	15 g

- Heat suet in skillet until fat separates from connective tissue or heat vegetable oil for healthier cooking. Remove suet and brown sirloin on all sides.

- Pour sirloin and oil from skillet in large pot or roasting pan. Add ground chile peppers, 1 whole jalapeno and enough water to be about 2 inches (5 cm) above meat.

- Bring water to boil, reduce heat and simmer for about 2 to 3 hours. Stir occasionally and skim grease.

- Add garlic, paprika, cumin and 1 tablespoon (15 ml) salt, cover and simmer for additional 1 hour. Stir occasionally and skim grease.

- Check seasonings and if not hot enough, add whole jalapeno. Add masa harina if chili is too thin and simmer for additional 30 minutes to 1 hour. Serves 6.

TIP: Masa harina is a flour made from sun-dried or oven-dried corn kernels and is used to make corn tortillas.

Championship Chili

Real chili is worth the effort! Boy I mean!

Olive oil
3 - 3½ pounds stew
   meat   1.4 - 1.6 kg
1 onion, chopped
1 (15 ounce) can
   tomato sauce   425 g
10 - 12 tablespoons
   dried chile
   colorado*
   peppers, ground,
   seeded   65 - 80 g
1 - 2 tablespoons
   ground cumin   5 - 15 g
1 tablespoon oregano 15 ml
1 - 2 jalapenos
Crackers

- Brown stew meat and onion in a little oil in large pot or roasting pan.

- Add tomato sauce, ground chilies, cumin, oregano, 1 tablespoon (15 ml) salt and enough water to be 2 inches (5 cm) above meat and bring to a boil. Reduce heat and simmer for about 2 hours. Stir occasionally.

- Taste for seasonings and add whole jalapeno if more "hot" is needed. Simmer for an additional 1 hour.

- Serve immediately with crackers or wait until the next day to serve. Some people believe real chili needs time for flavors to blend. Serves 6 to 8.

TIP: Chiles Colorado are New Mexican Reds and are about 5 to7 inches (13 cm) long, about 1 to 2 (1.2 to 2.5 cm) inches wide, dark-red brown and slightly hot. If you have never ground dried chilies, use food processor, blender or coffee grinder. They will live through it and so will you. These are great peppers to use because you do not have to peel them when they are dry.

Big-Time Chili

*You know the chili's good
when it makes your nose run.*

2 onions, chopped
¼ cup olive oil   60 ml
3 pounds lean ground
    beef   1.4 kg
1 (15 ounce) can diced
    tomatoes   425 g
1 (6 ounce) can tomato
    paste   170 g
¾ teaspoon cayenne
    pepper   4 ml
4 - 6 tablespoons chili
    powder   25 - 40 g
2 teaspoons ground
    cumin   10 ml
1 tablespoon paprika   15 ml

- Saute onions in oil and brown
  ground beef in roasting pan.

- Mix in all remaining ingredients
  with 2 teaspoons (10 ml) salt
  and bring to a boil. Reduce heat
  and simmer for 3 hours.

- Stir several times and add water,
  if needed. Serves 6.

Venison Chili

¼ pound salt pork,
    quartered   115 g
2½ pounds ground
    venison   1.1 kg
2 onions, chopped
1 (15 ounce) can Mexican
    stewed tomatoes   425 g
¾ cup red wine   175 ml
2 teaspoons minced garlic 10 ml
3 tablespoons chili
    powder   30 g
¾ teaspoon dried oregano 4 ml
1 teaspoon ground cumin   5 ml

- Brown salt pork in soup pot over
  medium heat.

- Add venison and onion, cook
  over medium-high heat until
  venison browns and crumbles
  and stir often.

- Stir in tomatoes, wine, garlic,
  chili powder, oregano, cumin,
  1 cup (250 ml) water and a
  little salt.

- Bring to boil, reduce heat and
  simmer for 1 hour, stirring
  occasionally. Remove salt pork
  before serving. Serves 6.

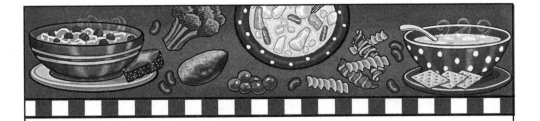

Perfect Pork Pleasers

Try these recipes loaded with ham, sausage and bacon and blended with hearty vegetables, beans, peas, rice and pasta.

Perfect Pork Pleasers Contents

Ham and Black Bean Soup

Half of the ingredients listed for this recipe are seasonings, so don't be scared about time and effort for this soup. It doesn't take much time to measure seasonings.

2 cups dried black beans	250 g
1 cup cooked, diced ham	280 g
1 onion, chopped	
1 carrot, chopped	
2 ribs celery, chopped	
3 jalapeno peppers, seeded, chopped	
2 (14 ounce) cans chicken broth	2 (400 g)
2 teaspoons ground cumin	10 ml
2 tablespoons snipped fresh cilantro	2 g
1 teaspoon oregano	5 ml
1 teaspoon chili powder	5 ml
½ - 1 teaspoon cayenne pepper	2 - 5 ml
1 (8 ounce) carton sour cream	230 g

- Wash beans, soak overnight and drain.

- Except for sour cream, place all ingredients and 1 teaspoon (5 ml) salt with 10 cups (2 L) water in large, heavy soup pot.

- Bring to boil, reduce heat and simmer for 3 hours or until beans are tender. Add more water as needed and stir occasionally. Make sure there is enough water in pot to make soup consistency and not too thick.

- Place few cups at a time in food processor (using steel blade) or blender and puree until smooth.

- Add sour cream and reheat soup. Serve in individual bowls. Serves 8.

Hearty Bean and Ham Soup

*What a great supper
for a cold winter night!*

1 (15 ounce) can sliced carrots,
    drained   415 g
1 cup chopped celery 200 g
1 cup seeded, chopped
    green bell pepper 140 g
¼ cup (½ stick) butter 60 g
2 - 3 cups cooked,
    diced ham   280 - 420 g
2 (15 ounce) cans
    navy beans with
    liquid   2 (425 g)
2 (15 ounce) cans
    jalapeno pinto
    beans with liquid 2 (425 g)
2 (14 ounce) cans
    chicken broth   2 (400 g)
2 teaspoons chili
    powder   10 ml

- Cook carrots, celery and bell pepper in soup pot with butter for about 8 minutes until tender-crisp.

- Add diced ham, navy beans, pinto beans, chicken broth, chili powder and a little salt and pepper. Boil and stir constantly for 3 minutes. Reduce heat and simmer for 15 minutes. Serves 8.

TIP: Cornbread is great with this and it's so quick and easy to make. If you want to fix it, just buy 2 (8 ounce/230 g) packages corn muffin mix. Add 2 eggs and ⅔ cup (150 ml) milk, mix it up and pour it into sprayed 7 x 11-inch (18 x 28 cm) baking pan. Bake according to package directions.

Pinto Bean Soup

2 (1 pound) packages
    dry pinto beans   2 (455 g)
1 smoked ham hock
    or 2 cups cooked,
    chopped ham   280 g

- Wash beans, cover with
  cold water in soup pot and
  soak overnight.

- Drain beans, cover with water
  and bring to boil.

- Add ham, reduce heat and
  simmer slowly for 3 to 4 hours.
  (You may need to add more
  water.)

- When beans are tender, remove
  2 to 3 cups (250 to 370 g) beans
  and smash with potato masher.

- Return to pot and season with
  salt. Serves 6.

Navy Bean Soup

*This soup tastes
great with cornbread.*

3 (15 ounce) cans navy
    beans with liquid   3 (425 g)
1 (14 ounce) can
    chicken broth   400 g
1 cup cooked,
    chopped ham   140 g
1 large onion,
    chopped
½ teaspoon garlic
    powder   2 ml

- Combine all ingredients with
  1 cup (250 ml) water in large
  saucepan and bring to boil.

- Simmer until onion is tender-
  crisp and serve hot. Serves 6.

Frijole Soup

1½ pounds dried pinto
   beans   680 g
5 slices thick sliced
   bacon, cut in pieces
2 onions, chopped
1 teaspoon garlic powder 5 ml
½ teaspoon thyme   2 ml
½ teaspoon oregano   2 ml
½ teaspoon cayenne
   pepper   2 ml
Flour tortillas
Butter

- Wash beans, place in large soup pot and cover with water. Soak overnight and drain.

- Cook bacon and onions in skillet for about 5 minutes.

- Transfer with pan drippings to soup pot. Bring to boil and add all seasonings.

- Lower heat and cook for 4 hours. Add hot water when liquid goes below original level.

- When beans are done, remove about half of beans and mash beans with potato masher or process in blender.

- Return to pot and add 1 tablespoon (15 ml) salt.

- Serve with hot flour tortillas and butter. Serves 4.

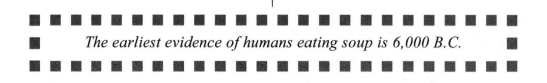

The earliest evidence of humans eating soup is 6,000 B.C.

Good Ol' Bean Soup

3 tablespoons olive oil 45 ml
1 cup shredded
   carrots 110 g
1 (16 ounce) package
   frozen, chopped
   onions and
   peppers 455 g
2 (14 ounce) cans
   chicken broth 2 (400 g)
2 (15 ounce) cans
   pinto beans with
   jalapenos with
   liquid 2 (425 g)
2 cups cooked, diced
   ham 280 g

- Combine oil, carrots, onions and peppers in soup pot and cook for 10 minutes.

- Add broth, pinto beans, ham and ½ cup (125 ml) water.

- Bring to boil, reduce heat and simmer for 15 minutes. Serves 6.

Ham Bone Soup

2 cups dried navy beans 525 g
½ pound ham hock 230 g

- Cover beans with water and soak overnight.

- Drain and pour beans in large soup pot with 6 cups (1.4 L) water.

- Cook with ham hocks for 2 to 3 hours or until tender.

- Season with a little salt and pepper. Serves 4.

Tomato and White Bean Soup

2 tablespoons olive oil 30 ml
1 onion, chopped
1 green bell pepper,
    seeded, chopped
1 (15 ounce) can diced
    tomatoes   425 g
2 (14 ounce) cans
    chicken broth   2 (400 g)
2 (15 ounce) cans
    navy beans,
    rinsed, drained   2 (425 g)
1½ cups cooked,
    cubed ham   210 g
½ cup chopped fresh
    parsley   30 g

- Combine olive oil, onion, bell pepper in large saucepan and saute for 5 minutes and stir constantly.

- Stir in tomatoes, broth, navy beans and ham and bring to boil. Reduce heat and simmer for 10 minutes.

- Pour into individual soup bowls and sprinkle parsley on top. Serves 4.

Easy Cannellini Soup

4 strips bacon
1 onion, chopped
1 red bell pepper,
    seeded, chopped
2 teaspoons minced
    garlic   10 ml
3 (14 ounce) can
    chicken broth   3 (400 g)
1 (15 ounce) can
    cannellini beans,
    drained   425 g
1 teaspoon dried
    parsley   5 ml

- Fry bacon in soup pot, drain and save drippings in soup pot. Crumble bacon and set aside. Add onion, bell pepper and garlic to drippings and saute for 5 minutes, stirring occasionally.

- Stir in chicken broth, beans, ½ teaspoon (2 ml) pepper, parsley and a little salt. Bring to boil, reduce heat and simmer for 20 minutes.

- Sprinkle crumbled bacon over each serving of soup. Serves 4.

Soup with an Attitude

1 (32 ounce) carton
   chicken broth   910 g
3 baked potatoes, peeled,
   grated
2 onions, finely chopped
3 ribs celery, sliced
1 (8 ounce) can peas,
   drained   230 g
1 (7 ounce) can green
   chilies   200 g
3 cups cooked, chopped
   ham   420 g
1 (16 ounce) package
   cubed Mexican
   Velveeta® cheese   455 g
1 (1 pint) half-and-
   half cream   500 ml

- Combine broth, potatoes, onions, celery, peas, green chilies and ham in soup pot.

- While stirring, bring to a boil, reduce heat to medium-low and simmer for 30 minutes.

- Add cheese and cook on medium heat, stir constantly until cheese melts.

- Stir in half-and-half cream and continue cooking until soup is thoroughly hot; do not boil. Serves 8.

To make a good base for your soup, you can use any of the following: canned soups (such as cream of mushroom soup), canned tomatoes, tomato juice, canned chicken broth, homemade stocks, commercial soup bases, clam or seafood broth and the addition of some bacon.

Cabbage-Ham Soup

1 (16 ounce) package
   cabbage slaw   455 g
1 onion, chopped
1 red bell pepper,
   seeded, chopped
1 teaspoon minced
   garlic   5 ml
2 (14 ounce) cans
   chicken broth   2 (400 g)
1 (15 ounce) can
   stewed tomatoes 425 g
2 cups cooked, cubed
   ham   280 g
¼ cup packed brown
   sugar   55 g
2 tablespoons lemon
   juice   30 ml

- Combine cabbage, onion, bell pepper, garlic, chicken broth and 1 cup (250 ml) water in large, heavy soup pot.

- Bring to boil, reduce heat and simmer for 20 minutes.

- Stir in tomatoes, ham, 1 teaspoon (5 ml) salt, brown sugar, lemon juice and a little pepper. Heat just until soup is thoroughly hot. Serves 6.

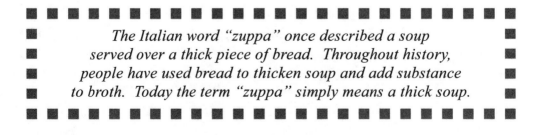

The Italian word "zuppa" once described a soup served over a thick piece of bread. Throughout history, people have used bread to thicken soup and add substance to broth. Today the term "zuppa" simply means a thick soup.

Spicy Bean Soup

1 (15 ounce) can
refried beans   425 g
1 (14 ounce) can
chicken broth   400 g
2 (4 ounce) cans
chopped green
chilies   2 (115 g)
2 cloves garlic,
minced
2 - 3 jalapeno chilies,
seeded, chopped
1 teaspoon chili
powder   5 ml
6 slices bacon
1 bunch green onions
with tops, chopped,
divided
5 ribs celery, chopped
1 bell pepper, seeded,
chopped
1 (8 ounce) package
shredded cheddar
cheese   230 g

- Heat and whisk refried beans and chicken broth in large saucepan.

- Add green chilies, garlic, jalapenos, ¼ teaspoon (1 ml) pepper and chili powder and stir well. Reduce heat to low and stir occasionally.

- Fry bacon in skillet until crisp and saute about three-fourths onions, celery and bell pepper in pan drippings until onions are translucent.

- Crumble bacon and add to bean soup.

- Add onions, celery, bell peppers and pan drippings and stir well.

- Bring to boil, reduce heat to low and serve immediately.

- Garnish with remaining onions and cheese. Serves 6.

Bonzo Garbanzo Soup

1 (16 ounce) package
   frozen diced onions
   and bell peppers   455 g
Olive oil
1 pound Italian
   sausage, cut up   455 g
1 (14 ounce) can beef
   broth   400 g
1 (15 ounce) can
   Italian stewed
   tomatoes   425 g
2 (15 ounce) cans
   garbanzo beans,
   rinsed, drained   2 (425 g)

- Saute onions and bell peppers in soup pot with a little oil.

- Add Italian sausage and cook until brown.

- Stir in beef broth, stewed tomatoes and garbanzo beans.

- Bring mixture to boil, reduce heat and simmer for about 30 minutes. Serves 6.

Lucky Pea Soup

Lucky Pea Soup is great on New Year's Day and brings good luck in the New Year.

1 onion, chopped
Olive oil
1 cup cooked, cubed ham   140 g
1 (15 ounce) can
   black-eyed peas with
   jalapenos with liquid 425 g
1 (14 ounce) can chicken
   broth   400 g
1 teaspoon minced garlic 5 ml
1 teaspoon dried sage   5 ml

- Saute onion in a little oil in large saucepan. Add ham, black-eyed peas, broth, garlic and sage and cook on high heat.

- Bring to boil, reduce heat and simmer and stir occasionally for 20 minutes. Serves 4.

Split Pea Soup

This is great for leftover ham.

1 (16 ounce) package	
dried green split peas	455 g
1 onion, chopped	
1 large potato, peeled,	
diced	
2 ribs celery, chopped	
1 cup cooked shredded	
or chopped ham	140 g
1 cup shredded carrots	110 g
1 teaspoon minced garlic	5 ml
Seasoned croutons	

- Sort and rinse peas and place in large, heavy soup pot. Cover with water 2 inches (5 cm) above peas and soak overnight.

- Drain, add 2 quarts (2 L) water, onion, potato, celery, ham, carrots, garlic and a little salt and pepper.

- Bring to boil, reduce heat, cover and simmer for 2 hours 30 minutes to 3 hours and stir occasionally. (If you happen to have a meaty ham bone, you can use that instead of chopped ham.)

- Cool slightly and process mixture in batches in blender until smooth.

- Return mixture to soup pot, cover and simmer for 5 minutes or until thoroughly hot.

- Garnish with seasoned croutons. Serves 6.

Split Pea and Tortellini Soup

⅓ cup dry split peas	65 g
2 tablespoons dried minced onion	8 g
1½ teaspoons dried basil	7 ml
1 tablespoon minced garlic	15 ml
½ cup shredded carrots	55 g
1 (10 ounce) can tomatoes and green chilies	280 g
¾ cup cheese-filled tortellini	180 ml
1 cup cooked, diced ham	140 g
2 (14 ounce) cans chicken broth	2 (400 g)

- Combine all ingredients with 1½ cups (375 ml) water in soup pot.

- Bring to boil, reduce heat and simmer for 45 minutes or until peas are tender. Serves 6.

Tomato-Bacon Soup

1 (10 ounce) can tomato soup	280 g
1 (14 ounce) can stewed tomatoes with celery and peppers	400 g
3 slices bacon, fried, drained, crumbled	

- Combine soup and stewed tomatoes in soup pot. Heat thoroughly.

- Pour into soup bowls, sprinkle bacon on top and serve hot. Serves 4.

Old-Fashioned Hoppin' John

2 (15 ounce) cans black-eyed peas with jalapenos with liquid	2 (425 g)
1 (14 ounce) can chicken broth	400 g
1 teaspoon minced garlic	5 ml
½ cup rice	50 g
2 onions, finely chopped	
1 red bell pepper, seeded, chopped	
1½ cups cooked, cubed ham	210 g
1 (8 ounce) package frozen mustard greens, coarsely chopped	230 g

- Combine peas, broth, 2 cups (500 ml) water, garlic, rice, onions and bell pepper in soup pot and bring to boil.

- Reduce heat and simmer, stirring occasionally, until rice is tender, for about 25 to 30 minutes.

- Stir in ham and greens and cook on medium heat for 5 to 10 minutes or until soup is thoroughly hot. Serves 4.

Soup That's Soul Food

3 (15 ounce) cans
   navy beans with
   liquid   3 (425 g)
2 onions, chopped
2 teaspoons minced
   garlic   10 ml
3 potatoes, peeled,
   cubed
2 cups cooked, diced
   ham   280 g
2 (14 ounce) cans
   chicken broth   2 (400 g)
1 (10 ounce) package
   frozen chopped
   turnip greens   280 g

- Place 1 can beans in shallow bowl and mash with fork. Spray large soup pot and stir in mashed beans, remaining cans of beans, onions, garlic, potatoes, ham, broth, turnip greens and a little salt and pepper. Bring to a boil and boil for 5 minutes; reduce heat to low and simmer for 45 minutes or until potatoes and greens are tender. Serve hot. Serves 6.

Potato-Sausage Soup

1 pound pork sausage
   links   455 g
1 cup chopped celery   100 g
1 cup chopped onion   160 g
2 (10 ounce) cans
   potato soup   2 (280 g)
1 (14 ounce) can
   chicken broth   400 g

- Cut sausage into 1-inch (2.5 cm) diagonal slices.

- Brown sausage in large heavy soup pot, drain and place in separate bowl.

- Leave about 2 tablespoons (30 ml) sausage drippings in skillet and saute celery and onion.

- Add potato soup, ¾ cup (175 ml) water, chicken broth and sausage.

- Bring to boil, reduce heat and simmer for 20 minutes. Serves 4.

Rich Cheese Soup

5 slices bacon
1 small onion, finely chopped
2 ribs celery, finely sliced
1 medium leek, halved lengthwise, sliced
2 (14 ounce) cans chicken broth   2 (400 g)
⅔ cup quick-cooking oats   55 g
1 cup shredded Swiss cheese   110 g
1 (8 ounce) carton whipping cream   250 ml

- Cook bacon in large saucepan until crisp, drain and crumble. Save drippings in saucepan.

- Cook onion, celery and leek in pan drippings over medium heat for 10 minutes and stir often.

- Add broth and oats. Bring to boil, reduce heat and simmer for 15 minutes. Cool slightly.

- Place half soup in blender and process until smooth. Repeat with remaining soup.

- Return all soup mixture to saucepan and stir in cheese and cream; heat until cheese melts. Do not boil.

- Ladle soup into bowls and sprinkle with crumbled bacon. Serves 4.

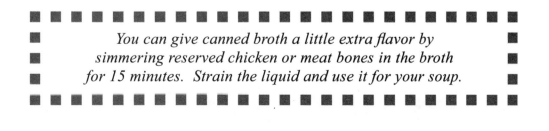

You can give canned broth a little extra flavor by simmering reserved chicken or meat bones in the broth for 15 minutes. Strain the liquid and use it for your soup.

Creamed Broccoli Soup

4 slices bacon
1 small onion, minced
3 potatoes, shredded
1 (10 ounce) package
    frozen chopped
    broccoli   **280 g**
¼ cup (½ stick) butter **60 g**
3 tablespoons flour   **20 g**
1 (1 pint) carton
    half-and-half cream **500 ml**

- Fry bacon in deep skillet, drain and set aside.

- With bacon drippings still in skillet, add onion, potatoes, 2 cups (500 ml) water and 1 teaspoon (5 ml) salt. Cover and cook for about 10 minutes.

- Add broccoli and cook for additional 5 minutes.

- In separate large saucepan, melt butter and add flour. Stir and cook until mixture bubbles. Gradually add half-and-half cream, cook and stir constantly until it thickens.

- Stir in potato-broccoli mixture and heat just until thoroughly hot. Crumble bacon and sprinkle on top of each serving. Serves 4.

Supper-Ready Potato Soup

1 (18 ounce) package frozen hash-brown potatoes with onions and peppers, thawed	510 g
2 (14 ounce) cans chicken broth	2 (400 g)
3 ribs celery, finely chopped	
2 (10 ounce) cans cream of chicken soup	2 (280 g)
2 cups milk	500 ml
2 cups cooked, chopped ham	280 g
2 teaspoons minced garlic	10 ml
1 teaspoon dried parsley flakes	5 ml

- Combine hash-brown potatoes, broth and celery in large soup pot and bring to boil. Reduce heat and simmer for 25 minutes.

- Pour in soup and milk and stir until mixture is smooth.

- Add ham, garlic, parsley and ½ teaspoon (2 ml) pepper.

- Bring to boil, stir constantly, immediately reduce heat and simmer for 10 minutes. Serves 6.

Bacon-Potato Soup

2 (14 ounce) cans
    chicken broth
    seasoned with
    garlic   2 (400 g)
2 potatoes, peeled,
    cubed
1 onion, finely
    chopped
6 strips bacon,
    cooked, crumbled

- Combine broth, potatoes and onion in large saucepan. Bring to a boil, reduce heat to medium-high and boil for about 10 minutes or until potatoes are tender.

- Season with a little pepper. Ladle into bowls and sprinkle with crumbled bacon. Serves 4.

Snap-Your-Fingers Potato Soup

2 (10 ounce) cans
    cream of potato
    soup   2 (280 g)
1 cup shredded
    cheddar cheese   115 g
3 tablespoons real
    bacon bits   10 g

- Heat potato soup with 1 cup (250 ml) water or milk in soup pot. Stir in cheese.

- Pour soup into soup bowls and sprinkle with bacon bits. Serves 4.

Green Chile Soup

5 slices bacon, cut into 1-inch pieces, divided	5 (2.5 cm)
1 onion, finely chopped	
2 ribs celery, finely chopped	
3 potatoes, peeled, cubed	
1 (7 ounce) can chopped green chilies	200 g
2 (14 ounce) cans chicken broth	2 (400 g)
1 (1 pint) carton half-and-half cream	500 ml

- Fry bacon pieces until half done in soup pot. Place half bacon in separate bowl and set aside.

- Add onion and celery to soup pot and cook on medium heat until onion is translucent.

- Add potatoes, green chilies, chicken broth, ½ cup (125 ml) water and ½ teaspoon (2 ml) each of salt and pepper.

- Cook on medium-low heat until potatoes are tender, about 15 minutes. To make soup a little thicker, mash some potatoes with fork against sides of pan.

- When ready to serve, pour in half-and-half cream and heat, but do not boil.

- Microwave remaining bacon until crisp. Sprinkle bacon on top of each serving to garnish. Serves 6.

Cowboy Sausage-Bean Soup

1 pound pork sausage	455 g
2 (15 ounce) cans pinto beans	2 (425 g)
2 (15 ounce) cans stewed tomatoes	2 (425 g)
1 onion, chopped	
¼ teaspoon garlic powder	1 ml
½ teaspoon thyme	2 ml
1 tablespoon chili powder	15 ml
¼ teaspoon dried coriander	1 ml
1 large potato, peeled, diced	
1 bell pepper, seeded, chopped	
1 (8 ounce) package cubed Velveeta® cheese	230 g
½ cup shredded Monterey Jack cheese	60 g

- Brown sausage in large, heavy soup pot and drain fat.

- Add beans, tomatoes, 1 quart (1 L) water, onions, 1 teaspoon (5 ml) salt, garlic powder, thyme, chili powder, coriander and ¼ teaspoon (1 ml) pepper.

- Bring to boil, reduce heat, Cover and simmer for 1 hour.

- Add potatoes and bell pepper, cover and simmer for additional 30 minutes or until potatoes are soft, but not mushy.

- Stir in Velveeta® cheese and heat just until it melts.

- To serve, sprinkle each serving with Monterey Jack cheese. Serves 6.

Sausage-Tortellini Soup

1 pound Italian
    sausage   455 g
1 onion, chopped
3 ribs celery, sliced
2 (14 ounce) cans beef
    broth   2 (400 g)
½ teaspoon dried
    basil   2 ml
1 (15 ounce) can
    sliced carrots,
    drained   425 g
1 medium zucchini,
    halved, sliced
1 (15 ounce) can
    Italian stewed
    tomatoes   425 g
1 (9 ounce) package
    refrigerated
    meat-filled
    tortellini   255 g
Mozzarella cheese

- Cook and stir sausage, onion and celery in soup pot on medium heat until sausage is light brown.

- Drain and stir in beef broth, 1½ cups (375 ml) water, basil, carrots, zucchini, tomatoes, tortellini and a little salt and pepper.

- Bring to boil, reduce heat and simmer for 20 minutes or until tortellini are tender.

- Ladle into individual soup bowls and sprinkle each serving with cheese. Serves 6.

Supper Sausage Soup

1 pound bulk Italian sausage	455 g
1 (16 ounce) package frozen onions and peppers	455 g
2 (15 ounce) cans stewed tomatoes	2 (425 g)
1 (4 ounce) can sliced mushrooms, drained	115 g
2 (14 ounce) cans beef broth	2 (400 g)
¾ cup hot salsa	200 g
1 teaspoon dried basil	5 ml
1 teaspoon sugar	5 ml
Shredded mozzarella cheese	

- Brown and cook sausage, onions and peppers in soup pot until sausage crumbles.

- Stir in tomatoes, mushrooms, broth, salsa, basil, sugar and a little salt and pepper.

- Bring to boil, reduce heat and simmer for about 15 minutes.

- Before serving, sprinkle a little cheese over each serving. Serves 6.

Salty soup? If your sauce, soup or stew is too salty, add a peeled potato into the pot, and it will absorb the extra salt.

Wild Rice and Ham Soup

1 (6 ounce) box long
grain-wild rice   170 g
1 (16 ounce) package
frozen onions and
bell peppers   455 g
1 (10 ounce) can
cream of celery
soup   280 g
2 (14 ounce) cans
chicken broth   2 (400 g)
2 cups cooked, diced
ham   280 g
2 (15 ounce) cans
black-eyed peas
with jalapenos
with liquid   2 (425 g)
1 (8 ounce) carton
sour cream   230 g

- Cook rice according to package directions.

- Combine rice, onions and bell peppers, celery soup, broth, ham and black-eyed peas in soup pot.

- Bring to a boil, reduce heat and simmer for 20 minutes.

- When ready to serve, stir in sour cream. Serves 6.

Southern Gumbo

This is great for leftover ham and no one will know it's a "leftover" meal.

2 tablespoons butter	30 g
2 tablespoons flour	15 g
1 (14 ounce) can chicken broth	400 g
1 (15 ounce) can diced tomatoes	425 g
1 cup cooked, shredded ham	140 g
2 cups fresh, sliced okra	200 g

- Mix butter and flour in large saucepan. Cook over medium heat and stir constantly until a paste-like roux turns light brown. Stir in broth, tomatoes, ham and okra and bring to a boil.

- Reduce heat to low and simmer for 25 minutes, stirring often, until gumbo thickens slightly. Serves 4.

Sausage-Vegetable Soup

1 pound bulk Italian sausage	455 g
2 onions, chopped	
2 teaspoons minced garlic	10 ml
1 (1 ounce) packet beefy soup mix	30 g
1 (15 ounce) can sliced carrots, drained	425 g
2 (15 ounce) cans Italian stewed tomatoes	2 (425 g)
2 (15 ounce) cans garbanzo beans, drained	2 (425 g)
1 cup elbow macaroni	105 g

- Brown sausage, onions and garlic in large soup pot. Drain and add 4 cups (1 L) water, soup mix, carrots, tomatoes and garbanzo beans. Bring to boil, reduce heat and simmer for 25 minutes.

- Add elbow macaroni and continue cooking for additional 15 to 20 minutes or until macaroni is tender. Serves 6.

Ham and Fresh Okra Soup

1 ham hock
1 (10 ounce) package
   frozen butter beans
   or lima beans   280 g
1½ pounds cooked,
   cubed ham or chicken 680 g
1 (15 ounce) can stewed
   tomatoes   425 g
3 cups small, whole okra 215 g
2 large onions, diced
Rice, cooked

- Boil ham hock in 1½ quarts
  (1.5 L) water for about
  1 hour 30 minutes in soup pot.

- Add remaining ingredients
  with a little salt and pepper and
  simmer for additional 1 hour.

- Remover ham hock and serve
  over rice. Serves 6.

Easy Pork Tenderloin Stew

*Cornbread or hot biscuits are
really good with this stew.*

2 - 3 cups cooked,
   cubed pork   280 - 420 g
1 (12 ounce) jar pork
   gravy   340 g
¼ cup chili sauce   70 g
1 (16 ounce) package
   frozen stew
   vegetables   455 g

- Combine cubed pork, gravy,
  chili sauce, stew vegetables and
  ½ cup (125 ml) water in stew
  pot.

- Boil for 2 minutes, reduce heat
  and simmer for 10 minutes.
  Serves 4.

Pancho Villa Stew

1 pound smoked sausage	455 g
3 cups cooked, diced ham	420 g
3 (14 ounce) cans chicken broth	3 (400 g)
1 (15 ounce) can diced tomatoes with liquid	425 g
2 (7 ounce) cans chopped green chilies	2 (200 g)
1 large onion, chopped	
1 teaspoon garlic powder	5 ml
2 teaspoons ground cumin	10 ml
2 teaspoons cocoa	10 ml
1 teaspoon dried oregano	5 ml
2 (15 ounce) cans pinto beans with liquid	2 (425 g)
1 (15 ounce) can hominy with liquid	425 g
1 (8 ounce) can whole kernel corn, drained	230 g
Flour tortillas or cornbread	

- Cut sausage into ½-inch (1.2 cm) slices.

- Combine sausage, ham, broth, tomatoes, green chilies, onion, garlic powder, cumin, cocoa, oregano and ½ teaspoon (2 ml) salt in roasting pan.

- Bring to boil, reduce heat and simmer for 45 minutes.

- Add pinto beans, hominy and corn and bring to boil. Reduce heat and simmer for additional 15 minutes.

- Serve with buttered flour tortillas or cornbread. Serves 8.

Hearty Ranch-Bean Stew

½ pound lean beef stew meat	230 g
1 pound pork loin, cubed	455 g
2 tablespoons olive oil	30 ml
1 (14 ounce) can beef broth	400 g
2 (15 ounce) cans ranch-style beans with liquid	2 (425 g)
2 (15 ounce) cans Mexican stewed tomatoes	2 (425 g)
1 (11 ounce) can Mexicorn®	310 g
1 green bell pepper, seeded, chopped	
1 (0.4 ounce) packet ranch dressing mix	10 g
1 teaspoon ground cumin	5 ml
1 ancho chile	
Crushed tortilla chips	

- Brown beef and pork meats in hot oil in heavy stew pot and season with a little salt and pepper. Add beef broth and heat to boiling. Reduce heat and simmer for 30 minutes.

- Add beans, tomatoes, corn, bell pepper, dressing mix, cumin, ancho chile and ½ cup (125 ml) water; simmer for about 20 minutes.

- Before serving, remove ancho chile. Serve in bowl with handful of crushed chips on top of each serving. Serves 6.

TIP: If you don't want to use an ancho chile, just add chili powder to taste. Ancho chiles are dried poblano chilies that are about 3 to 4 inches (8 to 10 cm) long and turn from bright green to dark red when dried. They are mild and a little on the sweet side as far as chilies go.

Pecos Pork Stew

2 pounds boneless
   pork shoulder,
   cubed   910 g
Olive oil
1 (16 ounce) package
   frozen chopped
   onions and
   peppers   455 g
2 cloves garlic,
   minced
¼ cup fresh chopped
   cilantro   5 g
3 tablespoons chili
   powder   30 g
2 (14 ounce) cans
   chicken broth   2 (400 g)
2 cups peeled, cubed
   potatoes   300 g
1 (16 ounce) package
   frozen corn   455 g
Cornbread

- Brown meat in a little oil in large roasting pan.

- Stir in onions and bell peppers, garlic, cilantro, chili powder, 1 teaspoon (5 ml) salt and chicken broth.

- Cover and cook on medium heat for about 45 minutes or until pork is tender.

- Add potatoes and corn. Bring to boil, turn heat down to medium and cook for additional 30 minutes. Serve with cornbread. Serves 6.

Southwest Pork Stew

2 tablespoons olive oil 30 ml
2 onions, chopped
1 green bell pepper,
    seeded, chopped
3 teaspoons minced
    garlic   15 ml
2 pounds pork
    tenderloin, cubed   910 g
2 (14 ounce) cans
    chicken broth   2 (400 g)
2 baking potatoes,
    peeled, cubed
2 (15 ounce) cans
    Mexican stewed
    tomatoes   2 (425 g)
1 (15 ounce) can
    yellow hominy,
    drained   425 g
2 teaspoons chili
    powder   10 ml
1 teaspoon ground
    cumin   5 ml
1 tablespoon lime
    juice   15 ml

- Place oil in stew pot and saute onion, bell pepper and garlic for 5 minutes.

- Add cubed pork and chicken broth and bring to boil. Reduce heat and simmer for 25 minutes.

- Add potatoes and cook for additional 15 minutes or until potatoes are tender.

- Stir in tomatoes, hominy, chili powder, cumin, lime juice and a little salt. Heat just until stew is thoroughly hot. Serves 6.

Polish Vegetable Stew

Olive oil
1 onion, sliced
2 carrots, peeled, sliced
1 bell pepper, seeded,
    chopped
2 (15 ounce) cans
    stewed tomatoes   2 (425 g)
2 (15 ounce) cans new
    potatoes, drained,
    quartered   2 (425 g)
1 pound Polish
    sausage, sliced   455 g
1 (9 ounce) package
    coleslaw mix   255 g

- Place a little oil in large stew pot. Cook onion, carrots and bell peppers for 3 minutes or until tender-crisp.

- Add tomatoes and ½ cup (125 ml) water; stir well.

- Stir potatoes and sausage into soup mixture. Bring to boil, reduce heat and simmer for 10 minutes.

- Stir in coleslaw mix and cook on medium heat for additional 8 minutes, stirring occasionally. Serves 6.

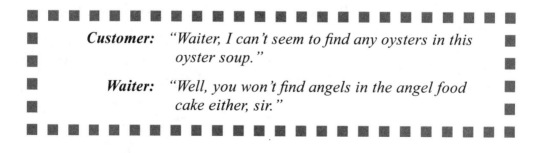

Customer: *"Waiter, I can't seem to find any oysters in this oyster soup."*

Waiter: *"Well, you won't find angels in the angel food cake either, sir."*

Black Bean Stew Supper

1 pound pork sausage
   links, thinly sliced 455 g
2 onions, chopped
3 ribs celery, sliced
Olive oil
3 (15 ounce) cans
   black beans,
   drained, rinsed   3 (425 g)
2 (10 ounce) cans
   diced tomatoes
   and green chilies   2 (280 g)
2 (14 ounce) cans
   chicken broth   2 (400 g)

- Place sausage slices, onion and celery in stew pot with a little oil, cook until sausage is light brown and onion is soft and drain.

- Add beans, tomatoes and green chilies and broth.

- Bring to boil, reduce heat and simmer for 30 minutes.

- Take out about 2 cups (500 ml) stew mixture, pour into food processor and pulse until almost smooth.

- Return mixture to pot and stir to thicken stew. Return heat to high until stew is thoroughly hot. Serves 6.

Ham and Sausage Stew

3 cups cooked, diced ham	420 g
1 pound Polish sausage, sliced	455 g
3 (14 ounce) cans chicken broth	3 (400 g)
2 (15 ounce) cans Mexican stewed tomatoes	2 (425 g)
1 tablespoon ground cumin	15 ml
Olive oil	
2 (15 ounce) cans navy beans with liquid	2 (425 g)
2 (15 ounce) cans whole kernel corn, drained	2 (425 g)
Flour tortillas	

- Combine ham, sausage, chicken broth, tomatoes, cumin and a little salt in large roasting pan.

- Add a little oil and cook on high heat for about 5 minutes.

- Add navy beans and corn, reduce heat and simmer for 35 minutes.

- Serve with warmed, buttered flour tortillas. Serves 8.

Did you know ice cubes love fat? Eliminate fat from soup by dropping ice cubes into your soup pot. As you stir, the fat will cling to the cubes

Turnip Greens Stew

2 cups cooked, chopped ham	280 g
2 (14 ounce) cans chicken broth	2 (400 g)
2 (16 ounce) packages frozen chopped turnip greens	2 (455 g)
1 (16 ounce) package frozen, chopped onions and bell peppers	455 g
1 (10 ounce) package frozen corn	280 g
1 teaspoon sugar	5 ml

- Combine all ingredients with 1 teaspoon (5 ml) pepper in large stew pot.

- Bring to boil; cover, reduce heat and simmer, stirring occasionally, for 25 minutes. Serves 6 to 8.

Southern Turnip Greens Stew

2 (16 ounce) packages frozen chopped turnip greens	2 (455 g)
1 (16 ounce) package frozen diced onions and bell peppers	455 g
2 cups cooked, chopped ham	280 g
2 (15 ounce) cans chicken broth	2 (425 g)

- Combine turnip greens, onions and bell peppers, ham, chicken broth and 1 teaspoon (5 ml) pepper in stew pot.

- Bring to boil, reduce heat, cover and simmer for 30 minutes. Serves 4 to 6.

Ham and Lentil Stew

1 (1 ounce) packet onion-mushroom soup mix	30 g
1 (14 ounce) can chicken broth	400 g
1 cup lentils, rinsed, drained	125 g
1 cup brown rice	185 g
2 cups chopped onion	320 g
2 cups chopped celery	200 g
2 (15 ounce) cans diced tomatoes with liquid	2 (425 g)
1 (15 ounce) can sliced carrots, drained	425 g
2 cups cooked, cubed ham	280 g
1 tablespoon apple cider vinegar	15 ml

- Combine soup mix, chicken broth, lentils, rice, onions, celery and 2 cups (500 ml) water in stew pot.

- Bring to boil, reduce heat and simmer for 45 minutes.

- Stir in tomatoes, carrots, ham and vinegar and cook on medium heat until mixture is thoroughly hot. Serves 6.

Posole

Posole is a traditional dish made famous in Jalisco, Mexico. Families pass recipes through generations and all have opinions about the ingredients for their special dish. This recipe is a faster version than the typical all-day soups or stews.

1 pound boneless pork shoulder, cubed	455 g
¼ cup flour	30 g
¼ cup olive oil	60 ml
1 clove garlic, minced	
1 onion, chopped	
1 (15 ounce) can pinto beans with liquid	425 g
1 (7 ounce) can chopped green chilies	200 g
1 - 2 teaspoons fresh, chopped cilantro	5 - 10 ml
½ teaspoon cayenne pepper	2 ml
2 (14 ounce) cans chicken broth	2 (400 g)
1 (15 ounce) can hominy, drained	425 g
1½ teaspoons dried oregano leaves	7 ml

- Dredge pork in flour and brown in oil in soup pot.

- Add garlic and onion, saute until onion is translucent and drain excess oil.

- Stir in beans, green chilies, cilantro, cayenne pepper and chicken broth.

- Bring to boil, cover and simmer for about 45 minutes.

- Stir in hominy, 1 teaspoon (5 ml) salt and oregano leaves and simmer for 15 to 20 minutes. Serves 6.

Quick-Step Posole

1½ - 2 pounds boneless pork shoulder, cubed	680 - 908 g
¼ cup flour	30 g
2 tablespoons olive oil	30 ml
2 onions, chopped	
1 clove garlic, minced	
2 ribs celery, chopped	
1 (8 ounce) can hominy, drained	230 g
1 (10 ounce) bottle red chili sauce	280 g

- Season pork with 1 teaspoon (5 ml) salt and ½ teaspoon (2 ml) pepper and dredge in flour on all sides.

- Heat oil in large saucepan and brown pork. Add onions, garlic and celery; cook until onions are translucent.

- Add hominy and red chili sauce to saucepan. Cover and cook on low for about 40 minutes or until pork is tender. Stir occasionally. Serves 6.

Easy Veggie-Ham Chowder

1 carrot, grated	
2 ribs celery, sliced	
1 onion, chopped	
1 (4.5 ounce) box julienne potato mix	130 g
3 cups milk	750 ml
2 cups cooked, cubed ham	280 g
Sharp cheddar cheese	

- Combine 2¾ cups (675 ml) water with carrot, celery, onion and potato mix in soup pot.

- Bring to boil, reduce heat, cover and simmer for 20 minutes.

- Stir in milk and packet of sauce mix from potatoes, mix well and bring to boil. Simmer for 2 minutes and stir in ham.

- Before serving, garnish with sharp cheddar cheese. Serves 8.

Ham and Corn Chowder

3 medium potatoes,
   cubed
2 (14 ounce) cans
   chicken broth,
   divided   2 (400 g)
2 ribs celery, chopped
1 onion, chopped
Olive oil
4 tablespoons flour   30 g
1 (1 pint) carton half-
   and-half cream   500 ml
½ teaspoon cayenne
   pepper   2 ml
1 (15 ounce) can
   whole kernel corn   425 g
1 (15 ounce) can
   cream-style corn   425 g
3 cups cooked, cubed
   ham   420 g
1 (8 ounce) package
   shredded
   Velveeta® cheese   230 g

- Cook potatoes with 1 can chicken broth in saucepan.

- Saute celery and onion in large soup pot with a little oil.

- Add flour and mix well on medium heat. Add second can broth and half-and-half cream. Cook, stirring constantly, until mixture thickens.

- Add potatoes, cayenne pepper, corn, cream-style corn, ham, cheese and a little salt and pepper. Heat slowly and stir several times to keep from sticking. Serves 8.

Ham Chowder

This is a real tasty way to use leftover ham. It has a great flavor!

1 cup sliced celery	100 g
½ cup chopped onion	80 g
2 tablespoons butter	30 g
3 cups shredded cabbage	210 g
3½ cups cooked, diced ham	490 g
2 (15 ounce) cans Mexican stewed tomatoes with liquid	2 (425 g)
1 (15 ounce) can whole kernel corn, drained	425 g
1 (15 ounce) can whole potatoes, drained, sliced	425 g
1 (14 ounce) can chicken broth	400 g
½ cup ketchup	135 g
¼ cup packed light brown sugar	55 g
½ teaspoon garlic powder	2 ml

- Saute celery and onion in butter in large roasting pan or soup pot over medium heat.

- Add remaining ingredients plus 1 cup (250 ml) water and ½ teaspoon (2 ml) salt and bring to a boil.

- Reduce heat, cover and simmer for 1 hour. Serves 6 to 8.

Caraway-Potato Chowder

1 (18 ounce) package frozen hash-brown potatoes	510 g
1 onion, chopped	
1 red bell pepper, seeded, chopped	
1 (14 ounce) can chicken broth	400 g
1 (10 ounce) can cream of celery soup	280 g
1 (1 pint) carton half-and-half cream	500 ml
2 teaspoons caraway seeds, crushed	10 ml
1½ cups cooked, chopped ham	210 g
½ teaspoon seasoned lemon pepper	2 ml

- Combine hash browns, onion, bell pepper and chicken broth in large saucepan.

- Bring to boil, reduce heat and simmer for 10 to 15 minutes or until potatoes are tender. Do not drain.

- Stir constantly on medium heat and add celery soup, half-and-half cream, caraway seeds, ham and lemon pepper.

- Heat just until thoroughly hot. Serves 8.

Women are more than twice as likely as men to cite soup as a typical lunch (10 percent versus 4 percent).

Potato-Ham Chowder

This is a great recipe to use when you have leftover ham!

3 medium potatoes
2 (14 ounce) cans
   chicken broth,
   divided   2 (400 g)
5 tablespoons butter   70 g
2 ribs celery, chopped
1 onion, chopped
2 (10 ounce) cans
   nacho cheese soup 2 (280 g)
1 (16 ounce) package
   frozen corn   455 g
1 (15 ounce) can
   cream-style corn   425 g
1 (1 pint) carton half-
   and-half cream   500 ml
3 cups cooked, cubed
   ham   420 g

- Peel potatoes, cut in small chunks and cook with 1 can chicken broth in medium saucepan.

- Melt butter in large soup pot and saute celery and onion.

- Add cheese soup and remaining can of chicken broth, stir constantly and cook until slightly thick.

- Add cooked potatoes with liquid and remaining ingredients plus 1½ teaspoons (7 ml) salt and ½ teaspoon (2 ml) pepper.

- Heat slowly and stir several times to keep from sticking. Serves 8.

TIP: This will only serve 6 to 8 because everyone will want a second bowl.

Rich Corn Chowder

8 ears fresh corn
8 slices bacon
1 small onion, chopped
½ red bell pepper,
**   seeded, chopped**
1 small baking potato,
**   peeled, cubed**
1 (1 pint) carton
**   half-and-half cream,**
**   divided**   **500 ml**
2 teaspoons sugar   **10 ml**
½ teaspoon dried thyme **2 ml**
1 tablespoon cornstarch **15 ml**

- Cut corn from cobs into large bowl and scrape well to remove all milk.

- Fry bacon in large soup pot over medium heat, remove bacon and save drippings in pan. Crumble bacon and set aside.

- Cook onion and bell pepper in drippings until tender.

- Stir in corn, potato, 1 cup (250 ml) water and a little salt and pepper. Bring to boil, cover, reduce heat and simmer for 15 minutes, stirring occasionally.

- Stir in 1½ cups (375 ml) half-and-half cream, sugar and thyme.

- Combine cornstarch and remaining cream and stir until smooth. Gradually add to corn mixture and stir constantly.

- Cook for 15 minutes, stirring constantly until soup thickens. Serves 6.

Veggie-Ham Chowder

1 large onion, chopped
3 ribs celery, sliced
Olive oil
3 cups shredded
    cabbage   210 g
3 cups cooked, cubed
    ham   420 g
2 (15 ounce) cans
    stewed tomatoes   2 (425 g)
1 (15 ounce) can
    whole kernel corn,
    drained   425 g
1 (15 ounce) can
    whole new
    potatoes, sliced   425 g
2 (14 ounce) cans
    chicken broth   2 (400 g)
1 cup thick-and-
    chunky salsa   265 g

- Saute onion and celery in large soup pot with a little oil over medium-high heat.

- Add remaining ingredients, bring to boil, reduce heat and simmer for 30 minutes. Serves 6.

Sausage Chowder

1 pound pork sausage 455 g
2 (15 ounce) cans
    kidney beans,
    rinsed, drained   2 (425 g)
1 (15 ounce) can
    diced tomatoes   425 g
1 medium potato,
    peeled, cubed
1 green bell pepper,
    seeded, chopped
1 onion, chopped
1 teaspoon minced
    garlic   5 ml
¼ teaspoon thyme   1 ml

- Brown and cook sausage in large soup pot and drain.

- Add beans, tomatoes, potatoes, bell pepper, onion, garlic, thyme and a little salt and pepper.

- Bring to boil, reduce heat and simmer for 1 hour. Serves 6.

Sausage-Bean Chowder

2 pounds pork sausage	910 g
1 (15 ounce) can pinto beans with liquid	425 g
1 (15 ounce) can navy beans with liquid	425 g
1 (15 ounce) can kidney beans, drained	425 g
2 (15 ounce) cans Mexican stewed tomatoes	2 (425 g)
2 (14 ounce) cans chicken broth	2 (400 g)
1 teaspoon minced garlic	5 ml

- Brown and cook sausage in soup pot and stir until sausage crumbles.

- Add all beans, tomatoes, broth and garlic and bring to boil.

- Reduce heat to low and simmer for 20 minutes. Serves 8.

Sausage and Corn Chowder

⅓ pound hot Italian sausage	150 g
2 (11 ounce) cans Mexicorn® with liquid	2 (310 g)
3 (14 ounce) cans chicken broth	3 (400 g)

- Remove casing from sausage, place in skillet, crumble and cook over medium heat.

- Stir in corn and chicken broth. Mix well and simmer for 10 minutes or until hot. Serves 6.

Green Chile-Corn Chowder

¼ pound bacon	115 g
1 medium onion, minced	
1 (15 ounce) can whole kernel corn with liquid	425 g
1 (15 ounce) can Mexican stewed tomatoes	425 g
2 - 3 fresh green chiles, roasted, peeled, seeded, chopped	
2 large baking potatoes, peeled, cubed	
1 teaspoon sugar	5 ml
1 teaspoon paprika	5 ml
1 (5 ounce) can evaporated milk	145 g

- Cut bacon into very small pieces and fry to crisp in skillet.

- Add onion and cook until translucent. Transfer to soup pot.

- Add corn, tomatoes, chiles, potatoes, sugar, ½ teaspoon (2 ml) salt, paprika and 3 cups (750 ml) boiling water.

- Cook on medium-low until potatoes are tender.

- Remove from heat and slowly stir in evaporated milk. Serve immediately. Serves 6 to 8.

Satisfying Seafood Delights

From rich, hearty chowders to Cajun-style seafood gumbos, these seafood specialties are special treats.

Satisfying Seafood Delights Contents

The word chowder comes from the French word "chaudiere," a caldron in which fishermen made their stews fresh from the sea. Chowder is a thick, chunky seafood or other thick, rich soup containing chunky food (such as corn chowder). Chowder can contain any of several varieties of seafood and vegetables. New England-style chowder is made with milk or cream and Manhattan-style chowder is made with tomatoes.

Spiked Crab Soup

1 (1 ounce) packet dry onion soup mix	30 g
1 (6 ounce) can crabmeat with liquid, flaked	170 g
1 (8 ounce) carton whipping cream	250 ml
½ cup white wine	125 ml

- Dissolve soup mix with 2 cups (500 ml) water in saucepan.

- Add crabmeat, crab liquid and whipping cream. Season with a little salt and pepper.

- Heat, but do not boil and simmer for 20 minutes. Stir in wine, heat and serve warm. Serves 6.

Carolina She-Crab Soup

4 cups milk	1 L
¼ teaspoon mace	1 ml
1 teaspoon grated lemon peel	5 ml
1 pound fresh crabmeat, flaked	455 g
1 (1 pint) carton whipping cream	500 ml
¼ cup (½ stick) butter	60 g
½ cup cracker crumbs	30 g
2 tablespoons sherry	30 ml

- Pour milk, mace and lemon peel in double boiler and simmer for 5 minutes.

- Add crabmeat, cream and butter and cook over low heat for 15 minutes.

- Stir in cracker crumbs a little at a time to get consistency desired and season soup with a little salt and pepper.

- Cover, remove from heat and set aside for 5 to 10 minutes so flavors blend. Add sherry before serving. Serves 6.

Oyster Soup

2 (14 ounce) cans
   chicken broth   2 (400 g)
1 large onion, chopped
3 ribs celery, sliced
1 red bell pepper,
   seeded, chopped
2 teaspoons minced
   garlic   10 ml
2 (1 pint) cartons
   fresh oysters,
   rinsed, drained   2 (500 ml)
½ cup (1 stick) butter   115 g
¼ cup flour   60 ml
2 cups milk   500 ml
1 tablespoon dried
   parsley   15 ml

- Combine broth, onion, celery, bell pepper and garlic in soup pot. Bring to boil, reduce heat and simmer, stirring occasionally for 30 minutes.

- Boil oysters in 2 cups (500 ml) water in saucepan for 2 minutes, stirring often or until edges of oysters begin to curl.

- Remove oysters with slotted spoon, coarsely chop half and set aside.

- Pour oyster stock into soup pot with vegetables.

- Melt butter in saucepan over medium heat, gradually whisk in flour and cook for 1 minute.

- Add flour mixture to soup pot and simmer, stirring occasionally over medium heat for 3 minutes.

- Stir in chopped oysters, milk, parsley and a little salt and pepper.

- Cook and stir occasionally over medium heat for 8 minutes or until mixture thickens.

- Stir in remaining whole oysters. Serves 6 to 8.

Seafood Bisque

¼ cup (½ stick) butter 60 g
1 (8 ounce) package
   frozen salad
   shrimp, thawed   230 g
1 (6 ounce) can crab,
   drained, flaked   170 g
1 (15 ounce) can
   whole new
   potatoes, drained,
   sliced   425 g
1 teaspoon minced
   garlic   5 ml
½ cup flour   60 g
2 (14 ounce) cans
   chicken broth,
   divided   2 (400 g)
1 cup half-and-half
   cream   250 ml

- Melt butter in large saucepan on medium heat. Add shrimp, crab, new potatoes and garlic and cook for 10 minutes.

- Stir in flour and cook, stirring constantly for 3 minutes.

- Gradually add chicken broth, cook and stir until mixture thickens.

- Stir in half-and-half cream and a little salt and pepper, stirring constantly and cook just until mixture is thoroughly hot; do not boil. Serves 6.

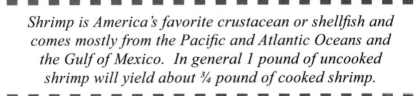

Shrimp is America's favorite crustacean or shellfish and comes mostly from the Pacific and Atlantic Oceans and the Gulf of Mexico. In general 1 pound of uncooked shrimp will yield about ¾ pound of cooked shrimp.

Creole Soup

2 tablespoons butter	30 g
1 (16 ounce) package frozen chopped onions and peppers	455 g
2 ribs celery,]sliced	
1 teaspoon minced garlic	5 ml
1 (6 ounce) package garlic, butter-flavored rice	170 g
2 (15 ounce) cans stewed tomatoes	2 (425 g)
1 teaspoon Creole seasoning	5 ml
1 (8 ounce) package frozen salad shrimp, thawed	230 g

- Melt butter and saute onions and peppers, celery, and garlic in large skillet.

- Stir in 1 cup (250 ml) water, rice, tomatoes and Creole seasoning and bring to boil.

- Reduce heat to medium and cook, stirring often, for 6 minutes.

- Add shrimp, cover and simmer for additional 5 minutes. Serves 6.

Use frozen vegetables such as peas, spinach or corn to cut prep time. Add them to assorted soups or puree them with broth, cream and sauteed onion, then simmer to make a smooth soup.

Low Country Crab Soup

1 onion, quartered
1 medium leek,
    white only
1 carrot, scraped, cut
    into 1-inch pieces   **2.5 cm**
3 ribs celery, cut into
    1-inch pieces   **2.5 cm**
¼ cup (½ stick)
    butter, divided   **60 g**
1 teaspoon minced
    garlic   **5 ml**
¼ cup flour   **30 g**
1 (14 ounce) can
    chicken broth   **400 g**
2 (1 pint) cartons
    half-and-half
    cream, divided   **2 (500 ml)**
1 tablespoon seafood
    seasoning   **15 ml**
¼ teaspoon cayenne
    pepper   **1 ml**
1 pound fresh lump
    crabmeat, flaked,
    drained   **455 g**
¼ cup brandy   **60 ml**
1 tablespoon chopped
    fresh parsley   **15 ml**

- Puree onion, leek, carrot and celery in blender.

- Melt 2 tablespoons (30 g) butter in soup pot over medium heat, add pureed vegetables and garlic. Cover and cook for 8 minutes, stirring often.

- Stir in flour, cook for 1 minute and stir often.

- Gradually stir in broth, 1 pint (500 ml) half-and-half cream, seasoning, cayenne pepper and a little salt. Cook for 10 minutes and stir occasionally.

- Melt remaining butter in small skillet, add crabmeat, toss gently over medium heat until thoroughly hot; stir in brandy.

- Stir crabmeat mixture, parsley and remaining half-and-half cream into vegetables in soup pot. Heat until thoroughly hot. Serves 6.

Crab Bisque

1 (10 ounce) can cream
   of celery soup   280 g
1 (10 ounce) can pepper-
   pot soup   280 g
1 (1 pint) carton half-
   and-half cream   500 ml
1 (6 ounce) can crabmeat,
   drained, flaked   170 g
⅓ cup sherry   75 ml

- Mix soups and half-and-half cream in saucepan.

- Stir in crabmeat and heat through.

- Just before serving, add sherry and stir. Serves 6.

Easy Oyster Stew

3 fresh green onions, finely
   chopped
2 tablespoons butter   30 g
1 (12 ounce) container
   oysters with liquor   340 g
1 (1 pint) carton
   whipping cream   500 ml
2 cups milk   500 ml

- Saute green onions in butter in stew pot.

- Add oysters, cream, milk and a little salt and pepper.

- Cook over low heat until oyster edges begin to curl and mixture is hot, but not boiling. Serves 6.

TIP: If you want a little snap to this stew, add cayenne pepper to taste.

Frogmore Stew

Frogmore Stew originated in South Carolina's Low Country and dates back many years. According to one story passed down through the years, an old fisherman gathered up whatever he could find to put in a stew. Other stories credit specific people on St. Helena Island with the invention, but there's no disagreement to the fact that Frogmore Stew is a combination of sausage, seafood and corn. Here's one version of the famous dish.

3 tablespoons seafood seasoning	**20 g**
3 pounds smoked link sausage, sliced	**1.4 kg**
3 onions, peeled, chopped	
1 lemon, sliced, seeded	
½ cup (1 stick) butter	**115 g**
6 ears corn, halved	
3 pounds large shrimp peeled	**1.4 kg**

- Combine about 2 gallons (8 L) water, seasoning, sausage, onions, lemon and a little salt and pepper in very large stew pot and bring to boil. Simmer for 45 minutes.

- Add butter and corn and cook for 10 minutes.

- Add shrimp, cook for additional 5 minutes and drain water. Serve immediately. Serves 8.

Fresh
Oyster Stew

2 (1 pint) cartons
   fresh oysters with
   liquor   2 (500 ml)
3 slices bacon
1 small onion,
   chopped
2 ribs celery, chopped
1 (4 ounce) can sliced
   mushrooms   115 g
1 (10 ounce) can
   cream of potato
   soup   280 g
3 cups half-and-half
   cream   750 ml
⅓ cup fresh chopped
   parsley   20 g

- Drain oysters and save liquor.

- Fry bacon in skillet until crisp, drain bacon and crumble. Set aside.

- Cook onion and celery in bacon fat in large skillet on medium heat until tender.

- Add mushrooms, soup, oyster liquor, half-and-half cream and a little salt and pepper. Heat over medium heat, stirring occasionally, until mixture is thoroughly hot.

- Stir in bacon and oysters and heat for additional 4 to 5 minutes or until edges of oysters begin to curl.

- Sprinkle with parsley. Serves 6 to 8.

Easy New England Clam Chowder

2 (10 ounce) cans New
   England clam
   chowder   2 (280 g)
1 (10 ounce) can
   cream of celery
   soup   280 g
1 (10 ounce) can
   cream of potato
   soup   280 g
1 (10 ounce) can
   French onion soup 280 g
1 (15 ounce) can
   cream-style corn   425 g
1 cup milk   250 ml

- Combine all ingredients
  in saucepan. Heat and stir.
  Serves 6 to 8.

Clam Chowder Snap

1 (10 ounce) can New
   England clam
   chowder   280 g
1 (10 ounce) can
   cream of celery soup 280 g
1 (10 ounce) can
   cream of potato soup 280 g
1 (6.5 ounce) can
   chopped clams,
   drained   175 g
1 soup can milk

- Combine all ingredients in
  saucepan. Heat and stir.
  Serves 6.

Three-Can Clam Chowder

1 (10 ounce) can New
   England clam chowder 280 g
1 (10 ounce) can cream
   of celery soup   280 g
1 (10 ounce) can cream
   of potato soup   280 g
1 soup can milk

- Combine all ingredients in saucepan and mix well.

- Heat thoroughly and serve. Serves 4.

Cod and Corn Chowder

8 slices bacon
1 pound cod, cut into
   bite-size pieces   455 g
2 large baking potatoes,
   thinly sliced
3 ribs celery, sliced
1 onion, chopped
1 (15 ounce) can whole
   kernel corn   425 g
1 (8 ounce) carton
   whipping cream   250 ml

- Fry bacon in large, heavy soup pot, remove bacon and drain. Crumble bacon and set aside.

- Drain fat from soup pot and stir in 2½ cups (625 ml) water, cod, potatoes, celery, onion, corn and a little salt and pepper. Bring to boil, reduce heat, cover and simmer for about 20 minutes or until fish and potatoes are done.

- Stir in cream and heat just until chowder is thoroughly hot. When serving, sprinkle crumbled bacon over each serving. Serves 6.

Crab-Corn Chowder

1 (1.8 ounce) packet
   dry leek soup mix 60 g
2 cups milk   500 ml
1 (8 ounce) can whole
   kernel corn,
   drained   230 g
½ (8 ounce) package
   cubed Velveeta®
   cheese   ½ (230 g)
1 (7 ounce) can
   crabmeat, flaked 200 g

- Combine soup mix and milk in large saucepan, cook over medium heat and stir constantly until soup begins to thicken.

- While still on medium heat, stir in corn and cheese and stir until cheese melts.

- Just before serving, add crabmeat and stir until thoroughly hot. Serves 6.

Oyster and Vegetable Chowder

¼ cup (½ stick) butter 60 g
3 (8 ounce) cans whole
   oysters with liquor 3 (230 g)
1 (16 ounce) package
   frozen broccoli
   florets   455 g
1 (10 ounce) package
   frozen corn   280 g
1 (1 pint) carton half-
   and-half cream   500 ml
1 cup milk   250 ml

- Melt butter in large saucepan and stir in oysters, broccoli and corn. Cook over medium heat and stir often for 12 minutes or until vegetables are tender.

- Stir in half-and-half cream, milk, 1½ teaspoons (7 ml) salt and ½ teaspoon (2 ml) pepper.

- Cook over low heat and stir often until mixture is thoroughly hot. Serves 6.

Seafood Chowder

3 onions, chopped
2 bell peppers, seeded,
   chopped
2 ribs celery, sliced
¼ cup olive oil   60 ml
3 tablespoons flour   20 g
3 (15 ounce) cans
   stewed tomatoes   3 (425 g)
1 teaspoon minced
   garlic   5 ml
1 teaspoon hot sauce 5 ml
2 pounds medium
   fresh shrimp,
   peeled   910 g
1 pound fresh lump
   crabmeat, flaked   455 g
1 (12 ounce) carton
   oysters, drained   340 g

- Saute onions, bell peppers and celery in hot oil in soup pot.

- Add flour and cook for 1 minute, stirring constantly.

- Stir in tomatoes, garlic, hot sauce and a little salt and pepper. Bring to boil, reduce heat and simmer for 15 minutes.

- Add shrimp, crabmeat and oysters to soup. Cover and simmer for 15 minutes. Serves 8.

Cauliflower-Crab Chowder

1 (16 ounce) package frozen cauliflower	455 g
¼ cup (½ stick) butter	60 g
¼ cup flour	30 g
1 (14 ounce) can chicken broth	400 g
1½ cups milk	375 ml
1 (3 ounce) package cream cheese, cubed	85 g
1 (2 ounce) jar chopped pimento, drained	60 g
1 teaspoon dried parsley	5 ml
1 (8 ounce) package refrigerated, imitation crabmeat, drained	230 g

- Cook cauliflower in ¾ cup (175 ml) water in large saucepan until tender-crisp.

- In separate saucepan, melt butter, stir in flour and mix well. Add broth, milk and cream cheese and cook, stirring constantly, until thick and bubbly.

- Add mixture to saucepan with cauliflower and stir in pimento, parsley and a little salt and pepper.

- Stir in crab and heat just until thoroughly hot. Serves 8.

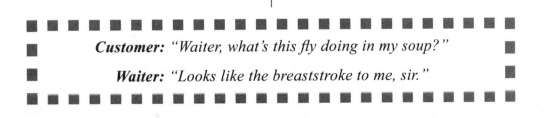

Customer: "Waiter, what's this fly doing in my soup?"

Waiter: "Looks like the breaststroke to me, sir."

Everybody's Seafood Gumbo

¼ cup (½ stick) butter   60 g
¼ cup flour   30 g
1½ - 2 pounds fresh
    okra, sliced   680 - 910 g
2 (15 ounce) cans
    whole tomatoes,
    chopped   2 (425 g)
½ cup minced onion   80 g
1 pound shrimp,
    peeled, cleaned   455 g
1 pound crabmeat,
    flaked, drained   455 g
1 pound fish filets,
    quartered   455 g
1 (1 pint) carton
    fresh oysters with
    liquor   495 g
Rice, cooked

- Melt butter in heavy skillet and add flour. Stir well over medium heat to make smooth, paste-like roux. When roux is rich brown color, add a little salt and pepper and mix well.

- Add 2 quarts (2 L) water, okra, tomatoes and onion. Cook on low for 20 minutes.

- Add all seafood and cook on medium-low for 30 minutes or until desired consistency. Serve over rice. Serves 8.

Seafood Gumbo

¼ cup olive oil	60 ml
½ cup flour	60 g
1 onion, finely chopped	
2 teaspoons minced garlic	10 ml
2 (10 ounce) packages frozen okra	2 (280 g)
1 (15 ounce) can diced tomatoes	425 g
¾ teaspoon cayenne pepper	4 ml
1 pound fresh, peeled, veined shrimp	455 g
1 pound crabmeat, flaked, drained	455 g
1 (1 pint) carton oysters, drained	495 g
3 fresh green onions, sliced	
Rice, cooked	

- Mix oil and flour in large soup pot. Cook over medium heat and stir constantly until paste-like roux turns light brown.

- Add onion, garlic, okra and tomatoes and cook on medium heat for about 10 minutes.

- Stir in 1 cup (250 ml) water, 2 teaspoons (10 ml) salt and cayenne pepper and simmer for 25 minutes.

- Add shrimp and crabmeat and simmer for 10 minutes.

- Add oysters and cook for additional 5 minutes.

- Stir in green onions and serve over rice. Serves 8.

Super Easy Gumbo

1 (10 ounce) can pepper-
   pot soup   280 g
1 (10 ounce) can chicken
   gumbo soup   280 g
1 (6 ounce) can white
   crabmeat, flaked 170 g
1 (6 ounce) can tiny
   shrimp, drained 170 g

- Combine all ingredients with
  1½ soup cans water in saucepan.

- Cover and simmer for 15 minutes.
  Serves 4.

Okra Gumbo

1 pound fresh okra,
   sliced   455 g
1 onion, chopped
½ cup (1 stick) butter 115 g
1 large potato, peeled,
   chopped
2 (15 ounce) cans
   diced tomato   2 (425 g)
1 (15 ounce) can
   whole kernel corn 425 g
Rice, cooked

- Saute okra and onion in butter
  in soup pot until light brown
  on outside.

- Add potato, tomatoes and
  corn and simmer for about
  30 minutes or until okra and
  potatoes are tender. Serve over
  rice. Serves 6.

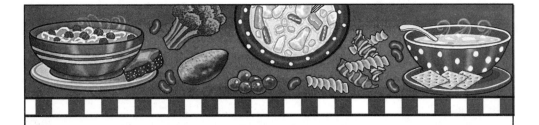

Veggie Meatless Masterpieces

Enjoy a rich, creamy bowl of piping hot cheese soup or maybe a nice bowl loaded with big chunks of potatoes and hearty vegetables. They're wonderful.

Veggie Meatless Masterpieces Contents

Veggie Meatless Masterpieces Contents

If you cook your pasta before adding it to your soup,
it doesn't bring all the starch with it and can be added
last so it doesn't get overcooked. You can even use
leftover pasta that you have stored in the fridge.

The Ultimate Cheddar Cheese Soup

1 cup finely chopped onion	160 g
1 red bell pepper, seeded, diced	
2 tablespoons butter	30 g
1 (16 ounce) package shredded extra sharp cheddar cheese	455 g
2 tablespoons cornstarch	15 g
1 (14 ounce) can chicken broth	400 g
1 (10 ounce) package frozen broccoli florets, thawed	280 g
1 (8 ounce) can sliced carrots	170 g
1 teaspoon Worcestershire sauce	5 ml
½ teaspoon garlic powder	2 ml
1 (1 pint) carton half-and-half cream	500 ml

- Saute onion and bell pepper in butter in large saucepan.

- Mix cheese and cornstarch in bowl.

- Pour broth and cheese-cornstarch mixture, a little at a time over onion and peppers and heat, stirring constantly, until cheese melts.

- Stir until smooth and add broccoli, carrots, Worcestershire sauce, ¼ teaspoon (1 ml) each of salt and pepper and garlic powder.

- Simmer and slowly add half-and-half cream while stirring. Do not boil. Serve immediately. Serves 6.

Old-Time Cheese Soup

¼ cup (½ stick) butter 60 g
1 small onion, finely
    chopped
2 ribs celery, finely
    chopped
½ cup shredded
    carrots   55 g
¼ cup flour   30 g
1 tablespoon
    cornstarch   15 ml
4 cups milk   1 L
2 (14 ounce) cans
    chicken broth   2 (400 g)
1 (12 ounce) package
    cubed Velveeta®
    cheese   340 g
1 tablespoon dried
    parsley   15 ml

- Melt butter in heavy saucepan on medium heat and saute onion, celery and carrots for about 10 minutes.

- Stir in flour and cornstarch and cook on low heat until bubbly.

- Gradually stir in milk and broth and blend into a smooth sauce.

- Add cheese; heat and stir constantly until mixture is smooth.

- Season with a little salt and pepper and stir in parsley. Heat, but do not boil. Serves 8.

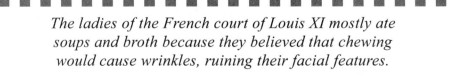

The ladies of the French court of Louis XI mostly ate soups and broth because they believed that chewing would cause wrinkles, ruining their facial features.

Country Cheddar Cheese Soup

¼ cup (½ stick) butter	60 g
2 ribs celery, chopped	
1 small onion, finely chopped	
1 bell pepper, seeded, chopped	
1 carrot, peeled, shredded	
1 (14 ounce) can chicken broth	400 g
½ cup (1 stick) butter	115 g
⅔ cup flour	80 g
1 quart milk	1 L
1 (8 ounce) package shredded sharp cheddar cheese	230 g

- Melt ¼ cup (60 g) butter and cook celery, onion, bell pepper and carrot in saucepan until tender and stir often.

- Stir in chicken broth, bring to boil, reduce heat and cook on low heat for 10 minutes.

- While vegetables cook, heat ½ cup (115 g) butter in large saucepan, stir in flour and cook, stirring constantly until bubbly.

- Remove from heat and gradually add milk. Cook over medium heat, stirring often, until soup thickens, but do not boil.

- Stir in cheese and heat until cheese melts.

- Stir in vegetable-broth mixture and heat just until hot. Serves 8.

Beer-Cheese Soup

¼ cup (½ stick) butter	60 g
¼ cup flour	30 g
1 (1 pint) carton half- and-half cream	500 ml
1 (12 ounce) can beer (not light)	340 g
1 (16 ounce) package cubed, Velveeta® cheese	455 g
¼ teaspoon cayenne pepper	1 ml
2 teaspoons marinade for chicken (Lea & Perrins)	2 ml
Hot sauce	

- Melt butter in large soup pot and add flour, stir until smooth and cook for 1 minute.

- Gradually add half-and-half cream and beer and cook over medium heat, stirring constantly, until thick.

- Add cheese and stir until cheese melts.

- Stir in cayenne pepper, marinade for chicken, a little salt and a dash of hot sauce, if you like. Heat while stirring and ladle into soup bowls. Serves 6.

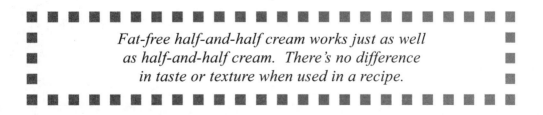

Fat-free half-and-half cream works just as well as half-and-half cream. There's no difference in taste or texture when used in a recipe.

Incredible Broccoli-Cheese Soup

This really is an incredible soup!

1 (10 ounce) package
    frozen chopped
    broccoli   **280 g**
3 tablespoons butter   **40 g**
¼ onion, finely chopped
¼ cup flour   **30 g**
1 (1 pint) carton half-
    and-half cream   **500 ml**
1 (14 ounce) can chicken
    broth   **400 g**
⅛ teaspoon cayenne
    pepper   **.5 ml**
1 (8 ounce) package
    mild Mexican, cubed,
    Velveeta® cheese   **230 g**

- Punch several holes in broccoli package and microwave for 5 minutes. Turn package in microwave and cook for additional 4 minutes. Leave in microwave for 3 minutes.

- Melt butter in large saucepan and saute onion, but do not brown.

- Add flour, stir and gradually add half-and-half cream, chicken broth, ½ teaspoon (2 ml) salt, ⅛ teaspoon (.5 ml) pepper and cayenne pepper.

- Stir constantly and heat until mixture is slightly thick. Do not let mixture boil!

- Add cheese, stir constantly and heat until cheese melts.

- Add cooked broccoli. Serve piping hot. Serves 4 to 6.

Creamy Chile-Cheese Soup

½ onion, minced
1 large tomato, minced
1 large, fresh green chile,
   peeled, seeded, minced
½ clove garlic, minced
3 tablespoons butter,
   divided   40 g
1 (14 ounce) can chicken
   broth   400 g
2 tablespoons flour   15 g
3 cups milk, divided   750 ml
1 (12 ounce) package
   shredded Monterey
   Jack cheese   340 g

- Saute onion, tomato, green chile and garlic until translucent in large skillet with 1 tablespoon (15 ml) butter.

- Pour in chicken broth, stir gently and pour into large saucepan.

- Melt 2 tablespoons (30 g) butter and add flour to skillet, stir constantly until mixture is smooth and beige in color. Stir out any lumps.

- Slowly pour in 1½ cups (375 ml) milk and stir constantly until sauce thickens slightly.

- Pour mixture into saucepan and continue cooking on low heat.

- Pour in remaining milk, ½ teaspoon (2 ml) salt, ¼ teaspoon (1 ml) pepper and cheese into saucepan and stir constantly. Simmer until cheese melts.

- Pour into soup cups and serve immediately. Serves 6.

Fiesta Tortilla Soup con Queso

3 (14 ounce) cans
   chicken broth   3 (400 g)
2 (15 ounce) cans
   stewed tomatoes   2 (425 g)
4 green onions with
   tops, chopped
1 (7 ounce) cans
   diced green chilies 200 g
1 clove garlic, minced
8 corn tortillas
2 tablespoons oil   30 ml
1 (16 ounce) package
   cubed Mexican
   Velveeta® cheese   455 g

- Pour chicken broth, tomatoes, onions, green chilies and garlic in large saucepan and heat on medium.

- Cut tortillas into long, narrow strips. Fry tortilla strips with hot oil in skillet for about 10 seconds or until strips are crisp. Remove from skillet and drain.

- Heat soup to boiling, reduce heat to low and stir in cheese.

- Serve in individual bowls and garnish with tortilla strips. Serves 8.

Herbs will have a more intense flavor if they are added when the soup is almost ready to serve.

Best-Ever Cheese Soup

¼ cup (½ stick) butter	60 g
1 bunch fresh green onions, sliced	
4 ribs celery, sliced	
3 (14 ounce) cans chicken broth	3 (400 g)
2 (10 ounce) cans cream of potato soup	2 (280 g)
1 (12 ounce) package shredded cheddar cheese	340 g
1 (8 ounce) carton sour cream	230 g

- Melt butter in large soup pot and saute onions and celery until tender.

- Add broth and bring to a boil, reduce heat and simmer for 20 minutes.

- Stir in potato soup and cheese and heat, stirring constantly until cheese melts. Stir in sour cream and heat, stirring constantly but do not boil. Serves 6 to 8.

Guacamole Soup

1 (18 ounce) can spicy tomato cocktail juice	510 g
½ cup chopped onion	80 g
2 avocados, peeled, seeded, diced, divided	

- Heat tomato juice and onion in soup pot for 5 minutes or until very hot.

- Stir in three-fourths of diced avocado and heat.

- Sprinkle remaining avocado on top of soup as a garnish and serve immediately. Serves 4.

Cream of Artichoke Soup

2 shallots, finely chopped
2 tablespoons butter   30 g
2 tablespoons flour   15 g
1 (14 ounce) can chicken
    broth   400 g
1¼ cups artichoke hearts,
    rinsed, drained,
    chopped   90 g
3 tablespoons fresh
    minced parsley,
    divided   10 g
1¼ cups half-and-half
    cream   310 ml

- Saute shallots in saucepan with butter until they are transparent.

- Add flour, stir to remove lumps and cook.

- Remove from heat and stir in chicken broth, artichoke hearts and 2 tablespoons (10 g) parsley.

- Return to medium heat and cook for 5 minutes.

- Puree mixture in blender. Strain pureed mixture through coarse sieve and return to clean saucepan.

- Heat on medium, slowly add half-and-half cream and blend thoroughly.

- Serve hot or cold. Garnish with remaining parsley, if desired. Serves 4.

Asparagus Soup

¼ cup (½ stick) butter 60 g
3 (14 ounce) cans
    chicken broth   3 (400 g)
¾ teaspoon garlic
    powder   4 ml
1 bunch green onions
    with tops, diced
1 large potato, peeled,
    cubed
½ (8 ounce) package
    cubed Velveeta®
    cheese   ½ (230 g)
1 (15 ounce) can cut
    asparagus   425 g
1 (8 ounce) carton
    sour cream   230 g
Real bacon bits

- Combine butter, broth, garlic, green onion and potato in large saucepan.

- Heat and cook for 15 minutes or until potatoes are tender.

- Add cheese and heat long enough for cheese to melt.

- Stir in asparagus. Fold in sour cream and heat (do not boil) just enough to make soup hot.

- Sprinkle bacon bits over top of each serving. Serves 6 to 8.

Some of the greatest artists in history were inspired by soup: Pablo Picasso painted "La Soup;" Vincent Van Gogh painted "Bowls and Bottles;" and James McNeill Whistler painted "Soupe a Trois Sous."

Creamy Asparagus Soup

1 onion, finely chopped
1 red bell pepper,
    seeded, chopped
2 tablespoons butter   30 g
2 (15 ounce) cans cut
    asparagus,
    drained   2 (425 g)
2 (10 ounce) cans
    cream of chicken
    soup   2 (280 g)
1 (1 pint) carton
    half-and-half
    cream   500 ml
1 teaspoon lemon
    juice   5 ml
¼ teaspoon dried
    tarragon   1 ml

- Saute onion and bell pepper in butter in soup pot.

- Add asparagus and blend in food processor until smooth.

- Return onion-asparagus mixture to soup pot and add chicken soup, half-and-half cream, lemon juice, tarragon and a little salt and pepper.

- Cook on medium-high heat and stir constantly until soup is thoroughly hot. Serves 6.

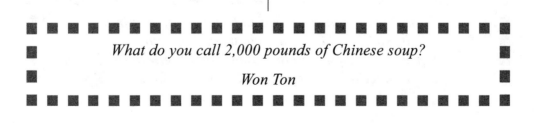

What do you call 2,000 pounds of Chinese soup?

Won Ton

At-Home Black Bean Soup

2 onions, finely chopped
3 teaspoons minced
    garlic   15 ml
Olive oil
3 (15 ounce) cans
    black beans,
    rinsed, drained,
    divided   3 (425 g)
2 (14 ounce) cans
    beef broth,
    divided   2 (400 g)
1½ teaspoons dried
    cumin   7 ml
2 teaspoons chili
    powder   10 ml
Shredded sharp
    cheddar cheese

- Saute onions and garlic in soup pot with a little oil and cook on medium heat for 5 minutes.

- Place 1 can beans and about ½ cup (125 ml) broth in food processor and process until beans are smooth.

- Transfer to soup pot and stir in remaining beans, remaining broth, cumin, chili powder and a little salt and pepper.

- Bring to boil, reduce heat and simmer for 15 minutes.

- Sprinkle cheese over each serving. Serves 4 to 6.

Black Bean Soup

1 pound dried black beans	455 g
1 (32 ounce) carton chicken broth	910 g
2 onions, chopped	
1 bell pepper, seeded, chopped	
1 tablespoon minced garlic	15 ml
2 tablespoons olive oil	30 ml
2 (10 ounce) cans tomatoes and green chilies	2 (280 g)
1 teaspoon chili powder	5 ml
⅓ cup lemon juice	75 ml
1 (8 ounce) carton sour cream	230 g

- Sort and rinse beans and place in soup pot. Cover with water 2 inches (5 cm) above beans. Bring beans to a boil, cover, remove from heat and let stand for 1 hour. Drain beans and return to soup pot.

- Add chicken broth to beans in pot, cover and cook over medium heat for 3 hours or until beans are tender. Stir occasionally. If beans get a little too dry, add ½ to 1 cup (125 to 250 ml) water.

- Saute onions, bell pepper and garlic in hot oil in large skillet until tender.

- Stir in tomatoes and green chilies, chili powder, lemon juice and a little salt and pepper and cook for additional 5 minutes.

- Process 2 cups (250 g) cooked beans in food processor until smooth.

- Stir remaining beans into soup pot and add onion-tomato mixture. Cook just until thoroughly hot, ladle into soup bowls and top each bowl with dollop of sour cream. Serves 8.

Ranchero Black Bean Soup

1 cup dried black beans	125 g
3 (14 ounce) cans beef broth	3 (400 g)
1 large bunch green onions with tops, chopped	
5 ribs celery, chopped	
3 cloves garlic, minced	
½ cup (1 stick) butter	115 g
½ cup rice	50 g
1 bay leaf	
6 peppercorns	
½ teaspoon cayenne pepper	2 ml

- Sort beans, rinse and soak in water overnight. Drain beans, transfer to large saucepan and cook for about 2 hours in beef broth.

- Saute onions, celery and garlic in butter in skillet until onions are translucent.

- Transfer onions, celery, garlic, rice, bay leaf, peppercorns, 1 teaspoon (5 ml) salt and cayenne pepper to beans.

- Cook for additional 2 hours or until beans are tender. (Add water if needed.)

- Remove bay leaf and peppercorns before serving. Serves 6.

TIP: *When serving, it is a nice touch to garnish with shredded cheese, sour cream or chopped green onions.*

Southwestern Bean Soup

Don't let the number of ingredients discourage you. Ask yourself this question, "Can I open cans?"

¼ cup (½ stick) butter 60 g
1 onion, chopped
1 bell pepper, seeded,
   chopped
2 teaspoons minced
   garlic   10 ml
2 (15 ounce) cans
   Mexican stewed
   tomatoes   2 (425 g)
1 (15 ounce) can
   pinto beans,
   drained   425 g
1 (15 ounce) can
   kidney beans,
   rinsed, drained   425 g
1 (15 ounce) can
   black beans,
   rinsed, drained   425 g
1 tablespoon chili
   powder   15 ml
¼ teaspoon ground
   coriander   1 ml
1 cup shredded
   Mexican
   4-cheese blend   115 g
1 cup shredded
   Monterey Jack
   cheese   115 g

- Melt butter in large saucepan on medium heat and cook onion, bell pepper and garlic for 5 minutes.

- Stir in tomatoes, all 3 cans beans, chili powder, coriander and a little salt and pepper.

- Bring to boil, reduce heat, cover and simmer for 25 minutes.

- Stir in Mexican cheese and cook over low heat, stirring occasionally just until cheese melts.

- Ladle into individual soup bowls and sprinkle Jack cheese over each serving. Serves 8.

Zesty Black Bean Soup

2 onions, finely chopped
Olive oil
3 teaspoons minced
    garlic   15 ml
1 tablespoon chili
    powder   15 ml
3 (15 ounce) cans
    black beans,
    divided   3 (425 g)
1 teaspoon ground
    cumin   5 ml
1 (14 ounce) can beef
    broth   400 g

- Saute onions in soup pot with a little oil, cook on medium heat for 5 minutes and stir in garlic and chili powder.

- Puree 1 can beans and add to onion mixture.

- Add remaining beans, cumin and beef broth. Bring to boil, reduce heat and simmer for 10 minutes. If you like, garnish with shredded cheese or salsa just before serving. Serves 6.

Black Bean-Corn Soup

1 onion, chopped
3 teaspoons minced garlic 15 ml
Olive oil
1 (28 ounce) can diced
    tomatoes   795 g
1 (15 ounce) can black
    beans, rinsed, drained 425 g
1 (10 ounce) package
    frozen corn   280 ml
½ cup cooked instant rice 85 g
1 red bell pepper, seeded,
    chopped
1 teaspoon dried cumin   5 ml

- Saute onion and garlic in a little oil in large soup pot for about 5 minutes.

- Stir in tomatoes, beans, corn, rice, bell pepper and cumin.

- Cover pot and bring to boil. Reduce heat and simmer for 15 minutes. Serves 6.

Creamy Broccoli Soup

2 tablespoons butter	30 g
½ cup chopped onion	80 g
1 (10 ounce) can cream of broccoli soup	280 g
1 cup milk	250 ml
4 ounces cream cheese, cubed	115 g
1 (8 ounce) package cubed Velveeta® cheese	230 g
1 (10 ounce) package frozen chopped broccoli	280 g

- Melt butter in large, heavy soup pot and saute onion for 5 minutes.

- Stir in soup, milk and cream cheese. Cook on medium-low heat and stir well until cream cheese melts.

- Add cheese, broccoli and a little salt and pepper. Cook on medium-low heat for 10 minutes or until cheese melts and soup is thoroughly hot. Serves 6.

Mexican Bean Soup

1 (15 ounce) can refried beans	425 g
1 (15 ounce) can pinto beans with jalapenos	425 g
1 (8 ounce) can tomato sauce	230 g
½ cup hot salsa	130 g
1 onion, chopped	
1 bell pepper, seeded, chopped	
2 (14 ounce) cans beef broth	2 (400 g)

- Combine all ingredients plus 1 cup (250 ml) water and mix well.

- Bring to boil in large soup pot, reduce heat and simmer for 30 minutes. Serves 6.

Garbanzo Bean Soup

2 tablespoons olive oil	30 ml
1 (16 ounce) package frozen chopped onions and peppers	455 g
2 teaspoons minced garlic	10 ml
½ teaspoon dried sage	2 ml
1 (15 ounce) can stewed tomatoes	425 g
2 (14 ounce) cans vegetable broth	2 (400 g)
1 (15 ounce) can garbanzo beans, drained	425 g
½ cup elbow macaroni	55 g
1 teaspoon Italian seasoning	5 ml
1 (5 ounce) package grated parmesan cheese	145 g

- Combine olive oil, onions and peppers and garlic in soup pot and cook, stirring often on medium heat for 5 minutes or until onions are translucent.

- Stir in sage, tomatoes, broth, garbanzo beans and a little salt and pepper and cook for 10 minutes.

- Stir in macaroni and Italian seasoning and cook for about 15 minutes or until macaroni is al dente (tender, but not overdone).

- Place about 1 heaping tablespoon (15 ml) parmesan cheese over each serving. Serves 6.

Broccoli-Cheddar Soup for Two

⅓ cup chopped onion	55 g
⅓ cup sliced celery	35 g
¼ cup (½ stick) butter	60 g
¼ cup flour	30 g
1 (14 ounce) can chicken broth	400 g
1½ cups milk or half-and-half-cream	375 ml
1 (10 ounce) package frozen chopped broccoli, thawed, cooked	280 g
⅔ cup shredded cheddar cheese	75 g

- Saute onion and celery in butter in large saucepan.

- Stir in flour and a little salt and pepper. Cook and stir constantly until smooth.

- Add broth and half-and-half cream and cook, stirring until mixture thickens.

- Add broccoli and simmer, stirring constantly, until mixture is thoroughly hot.

- Remove from heat, add cheese and stir until cheese melts. Serves 2.

In southern Italy, soup is said to relieve your hunger, quench your thirst, fill your stomach, clean your teeth, make you sleep, help you digest and color your cheeks.

At-Home Broccoli Soup

¼ cup (½ stick) butter 60 g
2 onions, finely
    chopped
3 tablespoons flour   20 g
3 (14 ounce) cans
    chicken broth   3 (400 g)
1 (16 ounce) package
    frozen chopped
    broccoli   455 g
1 cup shredded
    carrots   70 g
1 (5 ounce) can
    evaporated milk   145 g

- Melt butter in soup pot and saute onions for 5 to 6 minutes or until golden. Add flour and stir constantly until light brown. Stir in broth and bring to boil, reduce heat and simmer for 10 minutes, stirring constantly.

- Add broccoli and carrots and cook on medium heat for 10 minutes. Stir in evaporated milk and a little salt and pepper. Heat just until soup is thoroughly hot. Serves 6.

Broccoli-Wild Rice Soup

This is a hearty and delicious soup full of flavor.

1 (6 ounce) package
    chicken-flavored
    wild rice mix   170 g
1 (10 ounce) package
    frozen chopped
    broccoli   280 g
2 teaspoons dried
    minced onion   10 ml
1 (10 ounce) can cream
    of chicken soup   280 g
1 (8 ounce) package cream
    cheese, cubed   230 g

- Combine rice, rice seasoning packet and 6 cups (1.4 L) water in large saucepan. Bring to boil, reduce heat, cover and simmer for 10 minutes, stirring once.

- Stir in broccoli and onion and simmer for 5 minutes.

- Stir in soup and cream cheese. Cook and stir on low heat until cheese melts. Serves 6.

Cheese-Topped Broccoli Soup

3 (14 ounce) cans
   chicken broth   3 (400 g)
2 ribs celery, sliced
1 onion, chopped
1 medium baking
   potato, peeled,
   chopped
1 (16 ounce) package
   frozen chopped
   broccoli   455 g
1 (1 pint) carton half-
   and-half cream   500 ml
1 (5 ounce) package
   grated parmesan
   cheese   145 g

- Combine broth, ½ cup (125 ml) water, celery, onion and chopped potato in large, heavy soup pot.

- Bring to boil, reduce heat and simmer for 20 minutes or until vegetables are tender.

- Stir in broccoli and bring to boil, reduce heat and simmer for 15 minutes. Stir in half-and-half cream, ¼ teaspoon (1 ml) pepper and a little salt.

- Heat on medium, stirring constantly until soup is thoroughly hot. Ladle into individual soup bowls and sprinkle with parmesan. Serves 6.

Ninety-nine percent of all American households purchase soup each year, making it a $5 billion business.

Welcome Home Soup

2 cups fresh broccoli
   florets   140 g
4 - 5 large new (red)
   potatoes, chopped
1 bunch green onions
   with tops, chopped
2 (14 ounce) cans
   chicken broth   2 (400 g)
Sour cream

- Cook vegetables in chicken broth until tender and season with a little salt and pepper.

- Pour into blender and puree.

- Pour into soup bowls and garnish with dollop of sour cream. Serves 6 to 8.

Cream of Cauliflower Soup

1 onion, chopped
½ teaspoon garlic
   powder   2 ml
Olive oil
2 (14 ounce) cans
   chicken broth   2 (400 g)
1 large cauliflower,
   cut into small florets
1½ cups whipping
   cream   115 g

- Saute onion and garlic powder in a little oil.

- Stir in broth and boil. Add cauliflower and cook, stirring occasionally for 15 minutes or until tender.

- Process soup in batches in blender until smooth and return to pan.

- Stir in cream and add a little salt and pepper.

- Cook over low heat, stirring often until thoroughly hot. Serves 6.

Cream of Carrot Soup

1 small onion, chopped	
2 tablespoons butter	30 g
6 carrots, chopped	
2 tablespoons dry white wine	30 ml
2 (14 ounce) cans chicken broth	2 (400 g)
⅛ teaspoon ground nutmeg	.5 ml
1 (8 ounce) carton whipping cream, whipped	250 ml

- Saute onion in butter and add carrots, wine, chicken broth, nutmeg, ½ teaspoon (2 ml) pepper and a little salt in large saucepan.

- Bring to boil, reduce heat and simmer for 30 minutes or until carrots are tender.

- Pour half of carrot mixture into blender, cover and blend on medium speed until mixture is smooth. Repeat with remaining mixture.

- Return to saucepan and heat just until hot. Stir in cream. Serves 6.

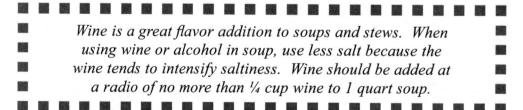

Wine is a great flavor addition to soups and stews. When using wine or alcohol in soup, use less salt because the wine tends to intensify saltiness. Wine should be added at a radio of no more than ¼ cup wine to 1 quart soup.

Cauliflower-Potato Soup

1 cup instant mashed potato flakes	60 g
½ cup finely chopped scallions, white part only	80 g
½ teaspoon caraway seeds	2 ml
2 (14 ounce) cans chicken broth	2 (400 g)
1 (16 ounce) package frozen cauliflower florets	455 g
1 (8 ounce) package shredded cheddar cheese, divided	230 g

- Combine 1½ cups (375 ml) boiling water, dry mashed potatoes, scallions, caraway seeds, 1½ teaspoons (7 ml) salt, 1 teaspoon (5 ml) pepper and chicken broth in soup pot.

- Bring to boil, reduce heat to medium and simmer for 10 minutes.

- Stir in cauliflower florets and cook for about 10 minutes or until cauliflower is tender.

- Stir in half cheddar cheese and serve in individual soup bowls with couple tablespoons cheese over top of each serving. Serves 8.

Cheesy Cauliflower Soup

1 (16 ounce) package
   frozen cauliflower
   florets   **455 g**
2 ribs celery, sliced
1 carrot, peeled, cut
   into chunks
1 onion, chopped
1 tablespoon instant
   chicken bouillon
   granules   **15 ml**
½ teaspoon lemon pepper **2 ml**
1 (8 ounce) carton
   whipping cream   **250 ml**
1 (8 ounce) package
   shredded Monterey
   Jack cheese, divided **230 g**

- Combine 2 cups (500 ml) water, cauliflower, celery, carrot, onion, chicken bouillon, ½ teaspoon (2 ml) salt and lemon pepper in large, heavy soup pot.

- Cover and cook for 1 hour or until vegetables are very tender.

- Pour half mixture into food processor and process until smooth. Repeat with remaining soup mixture.

- Return to soup pot and stir in cream and about three-fourths of cheese.

- Cook over medium heat, stirring constantly until cheese melts and mixture is thoroughly hot.

- Ladle into individual serving bowls and sprinkle remaining cheese over each serving. Serves 6 to 8.

Speedy Cauliflower Soup

2 (14 ounce) cans
  chicken broth   2 (400 g)
1 (10 ounce) can
  cream of potato
  soup   280 g
1 (4 ounce) can
  chopped pimento   115 g
1 (16 ounce) package
  frozen cauliflower   455 g
1 (1 pint) carton half-
  and-half cream   500 ml

- Combine broth, potato soup, pimento and ¾ cup (175 ml) water in large saucepan.

- Bring to boil, reduce heat and simmer for 10 minutes.

- Stir in cauliflower and cook for additional 20 minutes.

- Add half-and-half cream and heat just until soup is thoroughly hot. Serve 6.

Quick-and-Easy Corn Soup

2 (15 ounce) cans
  whole kernel corn   2 (425 g)
1 (10 ounce) can
  cream of potato
  soup   280 g
1 (14 ounce) can
  chicken broth   400 g
1 (8 ounce) carton
  whipping cream   250 ml
⅛ teaspoon cayenne
  pepper   .5 ml

- Combine corn, potato soup, broth, cream and cayenne pepper in saucepan.

- Cook on medium heat, stirring often until thoroughly hot. Serves 6.

Corn Soup Olé

2 (15 ounce) cans
    whole kernel corn 2 (425 g)
½ onion, chopped
2 tablespoons butter   30 g
2 tablespoons flour   15 g
2 (14 ounce) cans
    chicken broth   2 (400 g)
1½ cups half-and-
    half cream   375 ml
1 (8 ounce) package
    shredded cheddar
    cheese   230 g
1 (4 ounce) can
    chopped green
    chilies   115 g
Tortilla chips
Bacon bits

- Saute corn and onion in butter in soup pot.

- Add flour, ½ teaspoon (2 ml) salt and ¼ teaspoon (1 ml) pepper and cook for 1 minute.

- Gradually add broth and half-and-half cream while on medium-low heat. Cook and stir until it thickens slightly.

- Add cheddar cheese and green chilies. Heat but do not boil.

- Serve soup in individual bowls and stir in 4 to 5 crumbled, tortilla chips. Garnish with bacon bits. Serves 6.

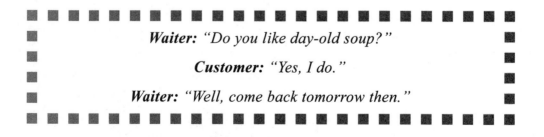

Waiter: "Do you like day-old soup?"

Customer: "Yes, I do."

Waiter: "Well, come back tomorrow then."

Creamy Corn Soup

¼ cup (½ stick) butter 60 g
1 (16 ounce) package
    frozen onions and
    bell peppers   455 g
1 (16 ounce) package
    frozen corn   455 g
1 (15 ounce) can
    cream-style corn   425 g
1 (10 ounce) can diced
    tomatoes and
    green chilies   280 g
2 (14 ounce) cans
    chicken broth   2 (400 g)
¼ cup flour   30 g
1 (1 pint) carton half-
    and half-cream   500 ml

- Melt butter and saute onions and bell peppers in soup pot on medium heat for 5 minutes.

- Stir in whole kernel corn, cream-style corn, tomatoes and green chilies and chicken broth. Bring to boil, reduce heat and simmer for 20 minutes.

- Mix ¼ cup (60 ml) water with flour in bowl and mix until they blend well. Stir into soup and heat, stirring constantly until soup thickens.

- Stir in half-and-half cream and heat soup, stirring constantly until thoroughly hot. Serves 8.

Quickie Corny Soup

3 strips bacon
1 small bunch green
   onions, minced
1 (15 ounce) can
   cream-style corn   425 g
1 (10 ounce) can cream
   of celery soup   280 g
1 soup can milk

- Fry bacon in large skillet and drain. Add onions to skillet and saute until translucent. Crumble bacon and sprinkle in skillet.

- Add cream-style corn, soup, milk and a little salt and pepper. Heat almost to boiling, stir often and pour into soup bowls. Serves 6.

TIP: If you want to add some type of garnish on top of the soup, fry some extra bacon and crumble it over the top or chop the green onion tops and sprinkle them on top. It looks and tastes great.

Quick Corn Chowder

2 baking potatoes, peeled,
   diced
½ cup shredded carrots   35 g
½ cup finely chopped
   onion   80 g
1 (15 ounce) can
   cream-style corn   425 g
1 (8 ounce) can whole
   kernel corn   230 g
1 (10 ounce) can cream
   of celery soup   280 g
1 cup milk   250 ml
1 (8 ounce) package
   cubed Velveeta®
   cheese   230 g

- Cook potatoes, carrots and onion in 1½ cups (375 ml) water in large saucepan for about 15 minutes or until potatoes are tender; do not drain.

- Stir in cream-style corn, whole kernel corn, soup, milk and a little salt and pepper. Heat and stir constantly until mixture is thoroughly hot; stir in cheese and serve. Serves 6.

Merry Split Pea Soup

1 (1 pound) package split peas	**455 g**
1 teaspoon dried parsley	**5 ml**
½ teaspoon garlic salt	**2 ml**
2 (14 ounce) can chicken broth	**2 (400 g)**
1½ cups chopped onion	**150 g**
1¼ cups chopped celery	**150 g**
¾ cup chopped carrots	**85 g**

- Soak peas overnight in water. Drain, rinse and pour 2 quarts (2 L) water over peas in large soup pot. Add parsley, garlic salt, chicken broth, onion, celery and ¾ teaspoon (4 ml) pepper.

- Cover and simmer for about 1 hour 30 minutes to 2 hours. Add carrots. Cover and simmer for additional 45 minutes. Serves 6.

Mexican-Style Minestrone Soup

1 (16 ounce) package frozen garlic-seasoned pasta and vegetables	**455 g**
1 (16 ounce) jar thick-and-chunky salsa	**455 g**
1 (15 ounce) can pinto beans with liquid	**425 g**
1 teaspoon chili powder	**5 ml**
1 teaspoon ground cumin	**5 ml**
1 (8 ounce) package shredded Mexican 4-cheese blend	**230 g**

- Combine pasta and vegetables with salsa, beans, chili powder, cumin and 1 cup (250 ml) water in large saucepan.

- Bring to boil, reduce heat, simmer for about 8 minutes and stir occasionally.

- When ready to serve, top each serving with Mexican cheese. Serves 6 to 8.

Italian Minestrone

1 (16 ounce) package
   frozen onions and
   bell peppers   455 g
3 ribs celery, chopped
2 teaspoons minced
   garlic   10 ml
¼ cup (½ stick) butter 60 g
2 (15 ounce) cans
   diced tomatoes   2 (425 g)
1 teaspoon dried
   oregano   5 ml
1 teaspoon dried basil 5 ml
2 (14 ounce) cans
   beef broth   2 (400 g)
2 (15 ounce) cans
   kidney beans,
   drained   2 (425 g)
2 medium zucchini,
   cut in half
   lengthwise, sliced
1 cup elbow macaroni 105 g

- Saute onions and bell peppers, celery, and garlic in butter for about 2 minutes in soup pot.

- Add tomatoes, oregano, basil and a little salt and pepper. Bring to boil, reduce heat and simmer for 15 minutes, stirring occasionally.

- Stir in beef broth, beans, zucchini and macaroni and bring to boil. Reduce heat and simmer for additional 15 minutes or until macaroni is tender. Serves 8.

Creamy Mushroom Soup

3 (8 ounce) packages
    fresh mushrooms   3 (230 g)
1 small onion, finely
    chopped
¼ cup (½ stick) butter,
    melted   60 g
½ cup flour   60 g
2 (14 ounce) cans
    chicken broth   2 (400 g)
1 (1 pint) carton half-
    and-half cream   500 ml
1 (8 ounce) carton
    whipping cream   250 ml
¼ cup dry white wine   60 ml
1 teaspoon dried
    tarragon   5 ml
2 teaspoons marinade
    for chicken
    (Lea & Perrins)   10 ml

- Coarsely chop and saute mushrooms and onion in butter in large soup pot.

- Add flour and stir until smooth.

- Add broth, half-and-half cream, whipping cream, wine, tarragon, Worcestershire sauce and about 1 teaspoon (5 ml) salt and stir constantly.

- Bring to boil, reduce heat to medium and cook for 20 minutes or until mixture thickens. Stir often. Serves 6.

Mushroom Soup

1 (10 ounce) can cream
    of mushroom soup   **280 g**
1 (14 ounce) can sliced
    mushrooms, drained   **400 g**
1 (14 ounce) can beef
    broth   **400 g**
1 (8 ounce) carton
    whipping cream   **250 ml**

- Combine all ingredients in medium saucepan.

- Mix well and heat thoroughly. Serves 4.

Microwave Mushroom Soup

1 (10 ounce) can cream
    of mushroom soup   **280 g**
1 (14 ounce) can beef
    broth   **400 g**
1 (4 ounce) can sliced
    mushrooms, drained   **115 g**

- Combine mushroom soup and broth in 2-quart (2 L) bowl and mix well. Microwave on HIGH for 1 minute and stir.

- Add sliced mushrooms and mix. Reduce heat to MEDIUM and microwave for additional 1 minute or until hot.

- Stir before serving. Serves 4.

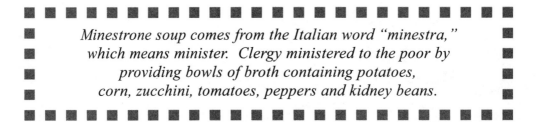

Minestrone soup comes from the Italian word "minestra,"
which means minister. Clergy ministered to the poor by
providing bowls of broth containing potatoes,
corn, zucchini, tomatoes, peppers and kidney beans.

Lunch-Ready Mushroom Soup

2 tablespoons butter	30 g
2 tablespoons flour	15 g
1 (14 ounce) can chicken	
broth	400 g
1 cup milk	250 ml
1 (8 ounce) package fresh	
mushrooms, sliced	230 g
1 teaspoon minced garlic	5 ml
1 teaspoon dried parsley	5 ml
1 teaspoon lemon juice	5 ml
1 cup half-and-half cream	500 ml

- Melt butter, stir in flour in large saucepan and cook, stirring constantly for 1 minute.

- Gradually stir in broth and milk, stirring constantly and bring to a boil.

- Add mushrooms, garlic, parsley, lemon juice and a little salt and pepper and simmer for 5 minutes.

- Add half-and-half cream and heat just until soup is thoroughly hot, do not boil. Serves 4 to 6.

Favorite Onion Soup

8 yellow onions,	
thinly sliced	
¼ cup (½ stick) butter	60 g
2 (32 ounce) cartons	
beef broth	2 (910 g)
8 slices French bread,	
crust trimmed,	
toasted	
8 slices Swiss cheese	

- Place onions and butter in large soup pot and saute onions until golden brown. Add beef broth and cook on medium heat for 1 hour.

- Just before time to serve, pour soup into 6 to 8 individual, ovenproof soup bowls, top with slices of toasted bread and cover with slices of cheese.

- Place bowls on baking sheet and place under broiler for 1 to 2 minutes or until cheese melts. Serve immediately. Serves 8.

Easy Veggie Soup

2 (14 ounce) cans
   beef broth   2 (400 g)
½ cup diced celery   50 g
1 (16 ounce) can
   mixed vegetables   455 g
1 bay leaf

- Mix all ingredients in large soup pot.

- Add 1½ cups (375 ml) water, 1 teaspoon (5 ml) each of salt and pepper and simmer for 45 minutes.

- Adjust seasonings, remove bay leaf and serve. Serves 4 to 6.

Tomato-French Onion Soup

1 (10 ounce) can
   tomato bisque
   soup   280 g
2 (10 ounce) cans
   French onion
   soup   2 (280 g)
Croutons
Grated parmesan
   cheese

- Combine soups and 2 soup cans water in saucepan. Heat thoroughly.

- Serve in bowls topped with croutons and sprinkle of cheese. Serves 4.

What is Dracula's favorite soup?

Scream of tomato

Creamy Parsley Soup

1½ pounds zucchini,
    chopped   680 g
2 (14 ounce) cans
    chicken broth   2 (400 g)
2 cups loosely packed
    parsley   120 g
1 (8 ounce) carton
    whipping cream   250 ml

- Combine zucchini and chicken broth in soup pot and cook until tender.

- Add parsley and cook for additional 5 minutes.

- Process in blender until smooth. Return to soup pot over low heat and slowly stir in cream. Season with a little salt and pepper. Serves 4.

Creamy Green Pea Soup

1 (16 ounce) package
    frozen green peas   455 g
1 cup milk   250 ml
1 (10 ounce) can cream
    of chicken soup   280 g
1 (14 ounce) can chicken
    broth   400 g
1 cup half-and-half
    cream   250 ml
Shredded Swiss cheese

- Cook peas according to package directions, place peas and milk in blender and blend to uniform consistency.

- Stir in soup, broth, ½ teaspoon (2 ml) pepper and a little salt. Bring to boiling (but do not boil), stirring constantly, reduce heat and simmer for 2 minutes.

- Stir in half-and-half cream and heat soup just until thoroughly hot. Sprinkle cheese over top of each serving. Serves 6.

Luncheon Pea Soup

1 cup instant mashed potato flakes	60 g
½ cup Italian salad dressing	125 ml
1 (16 ounce) package frozen peas and pearl onion	455 g
2 (14 ounce) cans chicken broth	2 (400 g)
½ cup sour cream	120 g

- Heat 1¼ cups (310 ml) water in large saucepan, stir in potato flakes and cook for 10 minutes. Stir in salad dressing, peas and onions.

- Transfer soup mixture to blender. Cover and blend small batches until smooth.

- Return blended mixture to saucepan and add chicken broth and ¾ teaspoon (4 ml) pepper. Bring to boil, reduce heat and simmer for about 15 minutes, stirring often.

- Stir in sour cream. Serves 4 to 6.

Quick-and-Easy Peanut Soup

¼ cup (½ stick) butter	60 ml
1 onion, finely chopped	
2 ribs celery, chopped	
2 (10 ounce) cans cream of chicken soup	2 (280 g)
2 soup cans milk	
1¼ cups crunchy peanut butter	360 g

- Melt butter in saucepan and saute onion and celery over low heat.

- Blend in soups and milk and stir.

- Add peanut butter, stirring constantly and continue to heat until mixture blends well. Serves 4 to 6.

Cream of Peanut Soup

½ cup (1 stick) butter	115 g
1 onion, finely chopped	
1 red bell pepper, seeded, chopped	
3 ribs celery, finely sliced	
¼ cup flour	30 g
2 (14 ounce) cans chicken broth	2 (400 g)
1½ cups peanut butter	740 g
1 (1 pint) carton half-and-half cream	500 ml
1 cup milk	250 ml

- Melt butter and saute onion, bell pepper and celery in large saucepan until vegetables are tender.

- Add flour, stir until smooth and cook for 1 minute.

- Gradually add chicken broth, stirring occasionally and cook on low heat for 25 minutes.

- Stir in peanut butter, ½ teaspoon (2 ml) pepper and a little salt.

- Gradually add half-and-half cream and milk, stir constantly and cook over low heat for 5 minutes or until thoroughly hot. Do not boil. Serves 6.

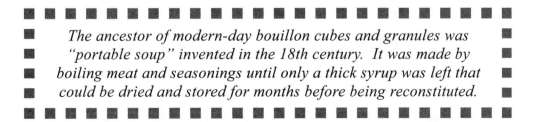

The ancestor of modern-day bouillon cubes and granules was "portable soup" invented in the 18th century. It was made by boiling meat and seasonings until only a thick syrup was left that could be dried and stored for months before being reconstituted.

EZ Potato-Pepper Soup

1 (18 ounce) package
    frozen hash-brown
    potatoes with
    onions and
    peppers   510 g
1 red bell pepper,
    seeded, chopped
2 (14 ounce) cans
    chicken broth   2 (400 g)
1 (10 ounce) can
    cream of celery
    soup   280 g
1 (10 ounce) can
    cream of chicken
    soup   280 g
1 (8 ounce) carton
    whipping cream   250 ml
4 fresh green onions,
    chopped

- Combine potatoes, bell pepper, chicken broth and 1 cup (250 ml) water in large saucepan and bring to a boil.

- Cover, reduce heat and simmer for 25 minutes.

- Stir in both soups and whipping cream and stir well. Cook until thoroughly hot.

- Garnish with green onions. Serves 6.

TIP: If you like, garnish with shredded cheddar cheese or diced, cooked ham.

Baked Potato Soup

5 large baking potatoes
¾ cup (1½ sticks) butter   170 g
⅔ cup flour   80 g
6 cups milk   1.4 L
1 (8 ounce) package
    shredded cheddar
    cheese, divided   230 g
1 (3 ounce) package real
    bacon bits   85 g
1 bunch fresh green
    onions, chopped,
    divided
1 (8 ounce) carton sour
    cream   230 g

- Cook potatoes in microwave or bake for 1 hour at 400° (205° C).

- Cut potatoes in half lengthwise, scoop out flesh and save. Discard potato shells.

- Melt butter in large soup pot over low heat, add flour and stir until smooth.

- Gradually add milk and cook over medium heat, stirring constantly, until mixture thickens.

- Stir in potatoes, half cheese, bacon bits, 2 tablespoons (10 g) green onions and a little salt and pepper. Cook until hot, but do no boil.

- Stir in sour cream and cook just until hot.

- Spoon into soup bowls and sprinkle remaining cheese and green onions over each serving. Serves 6.

Leek-Potato Soup

2 pounds baking potatoes, peeled, cubed	910 g
2 (14 ounce) cans chicken broth	2 (400 g)
¼ cup (½ stick) butter	60 ml
3 ribs celery, thinly sliced	
¾ cup thinly sliced leeks, white only	70 g
1 (1 pint) carton half-and-half cream	500 ml
¼ teaspoon ground nutmeg	1 ml

- Combine potatoes and chicken broth in soup pot. Bring to boil, reduce heat and simmer for 10 to 15 minutes or until potatoes are tender. Do not drain.

- Transfer half potato mixture to blender and blend until smooth. Repeat with remaining potato mixture and return to soup pot.

- Melt butter and cook celery and leeks in saucepan for about 5 minutes or until tender.

- Spoon into soup pot and add half-and-half cream, nutmeg and a little salt and pepper. Heat, stirring constantly until mixture is thoroughly hot. Serves 6.

In ancient Greece, soup made of peas, lentils and beans was sold in stalls on the street as perhaps the world's first fast food.

Potato-Cheese Soup

4 large potatoes, peeled,
  cubed
2 carrots, sliced
2 ribs celery, sliced
1 onion, finely grated
¼ cup (½ stick) butter   60 g
3 tablespoons instant
  chicken bouillon
  granules   45 ml
¼ teaspoon thyme   1 ml
½ teaspoon crushed
  rosemary   2 ml
¼ teaspoon garlic powder   1 ml
1 (1 pint) carton half-
  and-half cream   500 ml
1½ cups shredded
  cheddar cheese   170 g
3 slices bacon, cooked,
  crumbled

- Cook potatoes and carrots with enough water to cover vegetables in large saucepan.

- When done, mash with potato masher or mixer, but do not drain water off. Carrots will be chunky.

- Saute celery and onion in butter in small saucepan and add to mashed potatoes in large saucepan.

- Add all remaining ingredients except bacon and heat just until cheese melts.

- Lower heat, season with a little salt and pepper and simmer for 10 minutes.

- Serve with bacon pieces sprinkled over individual bowls of soup. Serves 6.

Garlic-Potato Soup

4 cups milk	1 L
1 (7 ounce) package roasted-garlic instant mashed potatoes	200 g
1 (10 ounce) can cream of celery soup	280 g
1 (8 ounce) package shredded sharp cheddar cheese, divided	230 g
1 (4 ounce) can chopped pimento	115 g

- Combine milk and 3 cups (750 ml) water in soup pot and bring to a boil. Remove from heat, add instant potato mix and stir with whisk until they mix well. Stir in celery soup and mix well.

- Stir in half cheese, pimento and ½ teaspoon (2 ml) pepper and stir until cheese melts. Ladle into individual bowls and sprinkle remaining cheese on top of each serving. Serves 6.

Easy Potato Soup

1 (18 ounce) package frozen hash-brown potatoes	510 g
1 cup chopped onion	160 g
1 (14 ounce) can chicken broth	400 g
1 (10 ounce) can cream of celery soup	280 g
1 (10 ounce) can cream of chicken soup	280 g
2 cups milk	500 ml

- Combine potatoes, onion and 2 cups (500 ml) water in large saucepan and bring to boil.

- Cover, reduce heat and simmer for 30 minutes.

- Stir in broth, soups and milk and heat thoroughly. Serves 8.

Pumpkin Soup

1 (8 ounce) package fresh mushrooms, sliced	230 g
3 tablespoons butter	40 g
¼ cup flour	30 g
2 (14 ounce) cans vegetable broth	2 (400 g)
1 (15 ounce) can cooked pumpkin	425 g
1 (1 pint) carton half-and-half cream	500 ml
2 tablespoons honey	45 g
2 tablespoons sugar	25 g
½ teaspoon curry powder	2 ml
¼ teaspoon ground nutmeg	1 ml

- Saute mushrooms in butter in large saucepan.

- Add flour, stir well and gradually add broth. Boil and cook for 2 minutes or until mixture thickens.

- Stir in pumpkin, half-and-half cream, honey, sugar, curry powder and nutmeg.

- Stir constantly until soup is thoroughly hot. Serves 6.

TIP: If you have some sour cream, a dollop of sour cream on top of soup is a very nice garnish.

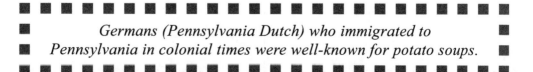

Germans (Pennsylvania Dutch) who immigrated to Pennsylvania in colonial times were well-known for potato soups.

Spinach Soup

2 (10 ounce) packages frozen chopped spinach, cooked	2 (280 g)
2 (10 ounce) cans cream of mushroom soup	2 (280 g)
1 cup half-and-half cream	250 ml
2 (14 ounce) can chicken broth	2 (400 g)

- Puree spinach, mushroom soup and half-and-half cream in blender in batches.

- Place spinach mixture and chicken broth in saucepan and heat on medium until thoroughly hot.

- Reduce heat to low and simmer for 10 minutes. Serve hot or cold. Serves 6.

Quick Spinach-Rice Soup

3 (14 ounce) cans chicken broth	3 (400 g)
2 (12 ounce) packages frozen creamed spinach, thawed	2 (340 g)
1 (10 ounce) can cream of onion soup	280 g
1 (4 ounce) can chopped pimento	115 g
½ cup instant rice	50 g

- Combine broth, spinach, soup, pimento, rice and a little salt and pepper in soup pot.

- Bring to boil, reduce heat and simmer for 10 minutes. Serve 6.

Zesty
Squash Soup

2 tablespoons butter   30 g
1 onion, finely
    chopped
2 tablespoons flour   15 g
2 (16 ounce) packages
    frozen yellow
    squash, thawed   2 (455 g)
1 (32 ounce) carton
    chicken broth   910 g
1 (7 ounce) can
    chopped green
    chilies   200 g
¾ cup whipping
    cream   175 ml

- Melt butter and saute onion in large soup pot for 3 minutes, stirring constantly.

- Stir in flour and cook for 1 minute.

- Add yellow squash, broth, ½ cup (125 ml) water, green chilies and a little salt and pepper. Bring to boil, reduce heat and simmer for 25 minutes.

- Puree soup in batches in blender until mixture is smooth.

- Return pureed soup to pot, add whipping cream and heat just until soup is thoroughly hot. Serves 6 to 8.

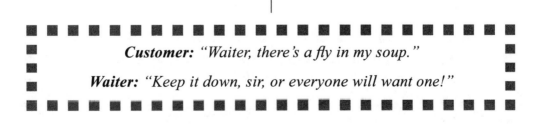

Customer: *"Waiter, there's a fly in my soup."*

Waiter: *"Keep it down, sir, or everyone will want one!"*

Johnny Appleseed's Squash Soup

1 small butternut
   squash
3 tart green apples
1 medium onion,
   chopped
¼ teaspoon dried
   rosemary   1 ml
¼ teaspoon dried
   marjoram   1 ml
3 (14 ounce) cans
   chicken broth   3 (400 g)
2 slices white bread
¼ cup whipping
   cream   60 ml

- Cut butternut squash in half and scoop out seeds.

- Peel, core and chop apples.

- Combine all ingredients except cream in large saucepan. Bring to boil, reduce heat and simmer for 45 minutes.

- Remove butternut squash, scoop out flesh from peel and discard peel.

- Add flesh back to mixture and puree in blender until smooth.

- Return mixture to saucepan and bring to boil. Just before serving, mix in cream. Serves 6.

TIP: By adding a bit more cream, this soup also tastes great cold.

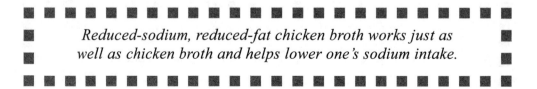

Reduced-sodium, reduced-fat chicken broth works just as well as chicken broth and helps lower one's sodium intake.

Creamy Butternut Soup

4 cups cooked, mashed butternut squash	450 g
2 (14 ounce) cans chicken broth	2 (400 g)
½ teaspoon sugar	2 ml
1 (8 ounce) carton whipping cream, divided	250 ml
¼ teaspoon ground nutmeg	1 ml

- Combine mashed squash, broth, sugar and a little salt in saucepan. Boil and gradually stir in half of whipping cream. Cook until thoroughly hot.

- Beat remaining whipping cream. When ready to serve, place dollop of whipped cream on soup and sprinkle with nutmeg. Serves 4.

TIP: It takes about 3 to 4 butternut squash to yield 4 cups (450 g).

Cream of Zucchini Soup

1 pound fresh zucchini, grated	455 g
1 onion, chopped	
1 (14 ounce) can chicken broth	400 g
½ teaspoon sweet basil	2 ml
1 (1 pint) carton half-and-half cream, divided	500 ml

- Combine zucchini, onion, broth, basil and a little salt and pepper in saucepan.

- Bring to a boil and simmer until soft. Place in food processor and puree.

- Gradually add ½ cup (155 g) half-and-half cream and blend.

- Return zucchini mixture to saucepan and add remaining half-and-half cream. Heat, but do not boil. Serves 4 to 6.

Zesty Zucchini Soup

¼ cup (½ stick) butter 60 g
3 cups coarsely
    chopped
    zucchini   370 g
2 ribs celery, thinly
    sliced
1½ teaspoons Italian
    seasoning   7 ml
½ - 1 teaspoon curry
    powder   2 - 5 ml
1 (10 ounce) can
    cream of potato
    soup   280 g
1 (10 ounce) can
    French onion
    soup   280 g
2 cups milk   500 ml

- Melt butter in soup pot and cook on medium-low heat.

- Add zucchini, celery, Italian seasoning and curry powder and stir constantly for 5 minutes.

- Stir in potato soup, onion soup and milk. Bring to boil, reduce heat and simmer for about 10 minutes. Serves 6.

TIP: If you want to serve with a nice garnish, place croutons and chopped green onions on top.

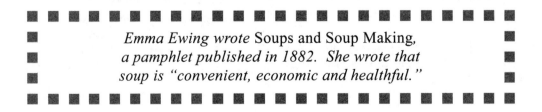

Emma Ewing wrote Soups and Soup Making, *a pamphlet published in 1882. She wrote that soup is "convenient, economic and healthful."*

Homemade Tomato Soup

3 (15 ounce) cans whole tomatoes with liquid	3 (425 g)
1 (14 ounce) can chicken broth	400 g
1 tablespoon sugar	15 ml
1 tablespoon minced garlic	15 ml
1 tablespoon balsamic vinegar	15 ml
¾ cup whipping cream	175 ml

- Puree tomatoes in batches with blender and pour into large saucepan.

- Add chicken broth, sugar, garlic, balsamic vinegar and a little salt. Bring to a boil, reduce heat and simmer for 15 minutes.

- Pour in whipping cream, stir constantly and heat until soup is thoroughly hot. Serves 4.

TIP: If you want to fry some bacon or have some ready-cooked, crumbled bacon in the pantry, it would be great as a garnish. If you don't have time, don't worry about it. No one will miss it, if you don't use it.

Creamy Tomato Soup

¼ cup (½ stick) butter	60 g
1 onion, chopped	
2 (28 ounce) cans diced tomatoes with liquid, drained	2 (795 g)
2 tablespoons light brown sugar	30 g
2 tablespoons tomato paste	35 g
2 tablespoons flour	15 g
1 (14 ounce) can chicken broth	400 g
1 (8 ounce) carton whipping cream	250 ml

- Melt butter in large soup pot, saute onions for about 4 minutes and stir constantly.

- Add drained tomatoes, brown sugar and mixture of tomato paste and flour. Cook, stirring often on medium heat for 10 minutes.

- Gradually stir in broth and reserved tomato juice and simmer on low for 15 minutes.

- Puree soup in batches in food processor until mixture is smooth.

- Pour pureed mixture back into soup pot and heat to boiling.

- Immediately remove from heat. Stir in whipping cream and a little salt. Serves 6.

TIP: If you want a "snappy" soup with a little fire, just add some hot sauce or a little cayenne pepper. That will get their attention.

Tomato-Basil Soup

2 (10 ounce) cans tomato soup	2 (280 g)
1 (15 ounce) can diced tomatoes	425 g
2 teaspoons finely minced onion	10 ml
2½ cups buttermilk*	625 g
2 tablespoons chopped fresh basil	5 g

- Combine tomato soup, tomatoes, onion, buttermilk, basil and ¼ teaspoon (1 ml) pepper and a little salt in saucepan.

- Cook, stirring often for 8 minutes or until thoroughly hot. Serves 4.

TIP: To make buttermilk, mix 1 cup (250 ml) milk with 1 tablespoon (15 ml) lemon juice or vinegar and let milk stand for about 10 minutes.

Tomato-Ravioli Soup

1 (15 ounce) can stewed tomatoes	425 g
2 (14 ounce) cans chicken broth	2 (400 g)
¾ teaspoon dried Italian seasoning	4 ml
1 (12 ounce) packet refrigerated cheese ravioli	340 g
2 small zucchini, sliced	
4 fresh green onions, sliced	

- Combine tomatoes, chicken broth, ½ teaspoon (2 ml) pepper and Italian seasoning in large saucepan. Bring to boil, reduce heat and simmer for 5 minutes.

- Add ravioli and zucchini and bring to boil, reduce heat and simmer for 8 to 10 minutes or until ravioli are tender.

- Sprinkle a few sliced green onions over each individual serving. Serve 6.

Warm-Your-Soul Soup

3 (14 ounce) cans
   chicken broth   3 (400 g)
1 (10 ounce) can
   Italian-stewed
   tomatoes with
   liquid   280 g
½ cup chopped onion 80 g
¾ cup chopped celery 75 g
½ (12 ounce) box
   fettuccini   ½ (340 g)

- Combine chicken broth, tomatoes, onion and celery in large soup pot.

- Bring to boil and simmer until onion and celery are almost done.

- Add pasta and cook al dente (firm but tender). Season with a little salt and pepper. Serves 4 to 6.

Fiesta Soup

1 (15 ounce) can
   Mexican stewed
   tomatoes   425 g
1 (15 ounce) can
   whole kernel corn 425 g
1 (15 ounce) can
   pinto beans
   with liquid   425 g
2 (14 ounce) cans
   chicken broth   2 (400 g)
1 (10 ounce) can fiesta
   nacho cheese soup 280 g

- Combine tomatoes, corn, pinto beans, broth and a little salt and mix well.

- Stir in soup and heat until thoroughly hot. Serves 6.

TIP: *If you want a heartier soup, just add 1 (12 ounce/340 g) can white chicken chunks.*

Zippy Tomato Soup

2 tablespoons butter	30 g
1 onion, chopped	
2 ribs celery, sliced	
1 bell pepper, seeded, chopped	
1 teaspoon minced garlic	5 ml
2 (15 ounce) cans Italian stewed tomatoes	2 (425 g)
1 (14 ounce) can vegetable broth	400 g
½ teaspoon cayenne pepper	2 ml
⅓ cup sour cream	80 g

- Melt butter in large saucepan and cook onion, celery, bell pepper and garlic over medium heat for 10 minutes or until vegetables are tender, but not brown.

- Stir in stewed tomatoes and transfer, in batches to food processor. Process until soup is almost smooth.

- Return soup mixture to saucepan and add vegetable broth, cayenne pepper and a little salt and pepper.

- Heat for 5 minutes or until soup is thoroughly hot. Stir in sour cream just before serving. Serves 4.

TIP: If you have some croutons in the pantry, throw a couple on top of each soup bowl before you serve. It's a nice touch, but not a "must-do".

Tomato-Tortilla Soup

8 corn tortillas, cut
    into strips
Olive oil
1 onion, chopped
½ cup finely chopped
    green bell pepper   75 g
½ teaspoon ground
    cumin   2 ml
2 teaspoons minced
    garlic   10 ml
2 (15 ounce) cans
    diced tomatoes   2 (425 g)
1 (4 ounce) can
    chopped green
    chilies   115 g
3 (14 ounce) cans
    chicken broth   3 (400 g)
½ bunch fresh
    cilantro, very
    finely chopped
1 (8 ounce) package
    shredded cheddar
    cheese   230 g

- Fry tortilla strips in hot oil in skillet and drain on paper towels.

- Saute onion, bell pepper, cumin and garlic in 2 tablespoons (30 ml) oil in large heavy soup pot.

- Add diced tomatoes, green chilies, chicken broth and cilantro and stir occasionally. Cook on medium heat for 20 to 25 minutes.

- When ready to serve, place some tortilla strips and shredded cheese in each bowl, pour soup into bowls and serve immediately. Serves 4 to 6.

TIP: If you want to make this a hearty, one-dish meal, add 2 cups (280 g) cooked, chopped chicken breasts.

El Paso
Tomato Soup

2 (10 ounce) cans
  tomato soup   2 (280 g)
1 (14 ounce) can
  chopped Mexican
  stewed tomatoes
  with onions   400 g
1 (10 ounce) can
  chopped tomatoes
  and green chilies   280 g
1 (14 ounce) can
  chicken broth   400 g

- Mix all ingredients plus 1 soup can water in saucepan.

- Heat to boiling and stir often. Reduce heat and simmer for 5 minutes. Serves 4.

Spicy
Tomato Soup

2 (10 ounce) cans
  tomato soup   2 (280 g)
1 (15 ounce) can
  Mexican stewed
  tomatoes   425 g
1 (4 ounce) can
  chopped green
  chilies   115 g
1 (10 ounce) can
  French onion soup 280 g
3 slices bacon, fried,
  drained, crumbled

- Combine tomato soup, stewed tomatoes, green chilies and onion soup in saucepan and heat thoroughly.

- To serve, sprinkle crumbled bacon on top. Serves 6.

Cheesy Vegetable Soup

2 large potatoes,
    peeled, diced
1 (16 ounce) package
    frozen onions and
    peppers   455 g
2 (14 ounce) cans
    chicken broth   2 (400 g)
1 (4 ounce) can sliced
    mushrooms,
    drained   115 g
1 (16 ounce) package
    frozen mixed
    vegetables   455 g
1 (10 ounce) can
    cream of celery
    soup   280 g
1 (12 ounce) package
    cubed Velveeta®
    cheese   340 g

- Combine potatoes, onions and peppers, chicken broth, and 2 cups (500 ml) water in large soup pot on medium heat.

- Cook for 15 to 20 minutes or until potatoes are tender.

- Stir in mushrooms, mixed vegetables and 1 teaspoon (5 ml) salt and cook for additional 10 minutes.

- Stir in celery soup and cheese, heat on medium-low and stir until cheese melts. Serves 6.

Swiss-Vegetable Soup

1 (1 ounce) packet vegetable soup mix	30 g
1 cup half-and-half cream	250 ml
1½ cups shredded Swiss cheese	160 g

- Combine soup mix and 3 cups (750 ml) water in saucepan and bring to boil.

- Lower heat and simmer for about 10 minutes.

- Add half-and-half cream and cheese, stir and serve hot. Serves 4.

Winter Sweet Potato Soup

2 tablespoons butter	30 g
1 cup sliced scallions, white part only	160 g
2 (15 ounce) cans sweet potatoes with liquid	2 (425 g)
2 (14 ounce) cans chicken broth	2 (400 g)
¼ teaspoon ground cinnamon	1 ml
½ cup half-and-half cream	125 ml

- Melt butter in large saucepan and saute scallions for about 5 minutes.

- Mash sweet potatoes slightly with fork and place in saucepan with scallions.

- Add chicken broth, cinnamon and a little salt. Bring to boil, reduce heat and simmer for 5 minutes.

- Stir in half-and-half cream. Soup may be served warm or chilled. Serves 4.

Southwest Chili and Tomatoes

4 scallions, sliced
4 teaspoons minced
    garlic   20 ml
2 teaspoons olive oil 10 ml
2 (15 ounce) cans
    diced tomatoes
    with liquid   2 (425 g)
1 (15 ounce) can
    pinto beans,
    rinsed, drained   425 g
¾ teaspoon cayenne
    pepper   4 ml
2 tablespoons chili
    powder   15 g
1 teaspoon ground
    cumin   5 ml
½ teaspoon coriander 2 ml
6 fresh sage leaves,
    snipped

- Saute scallions and garlic with olive oil in large saucepan over medium heat for about 3 minutes.

- Add tomatoes, beans, cayenne pepper, chili powder, cumin, coriander and a little salt.

- Heat chili to boiling, reduce heat, add sage and cook for 2 minutes.

- Remove sage leaves before serving. Serves 4.

Favorite Veggie-Lovers' Chili

2 onions, coarsely chopped	
2 tablespoons olive oil	30 ml
2 (15 ounce) cans diced tomatoes	2 (425 g)
⅔ cup medium-hot salsa	175 g
2 teaspoons ground cumin	10 ml
½ teaspoon dried oregano	2 ml
2 (15 ounce) cans pinto beans	2 (425 g)
1 green bell pepper, seeded, coarsely chopped	
1 red bell pepper, seeded, coarsely chopped	
1 cup halved baby carrots	135 g
4 cups hot cooked rice	380 g
1 (8 ounce) package shredded cheddar cheese	230 g

- Saute onion in oil in large soup pot.

- Add ½ cup (125 ml) water, tomatoes, salsa, cumin, oregano and a little salt and pepper.

- Bring to boil, reduce heat and simmer for 10 minutes.

- Stir in beans, bell peppers and carrots. Cover and cook over medium heat for 25 minutes and stir occasionally.

- Spoon rice into individual soup bowls and ladle chili over rice.

- Sprinkle generous amount of cheddar cheese on top of soup. Serves 6.

Vegetarian Chili

2 (15 ounce) cans
   stewed tomatoes   2 (425 g)
1 (15 ounce) can
   kidney beans,
   rinsed, drained   425 g
1 (15 ounce) can pinto
   beans with liquid   425 g
1 onion, chopped
1 green bell pepper,
   seeded, chopped
1 tablespoon chili
   powder   15 ml
1 (12 ounce) package
   elbow macaroni   340 g
¼ cup (½ stick)
   butter, sliced   60 g

- Combine tomatoes, kidney beans, pinto beans, onion, bell pepper, chili powder and 1 cup (250 ml) water in soup pot. Cover and cook on medium heat for 1 hour.

- Cook macaroni according to package directions, drain and add butter. Stir until butter melts.

- Add macaroni to chili and mix well. Serves 6.

Supper-Ready Vegetable Chili

1 (28 ounce) can diced
   tomatoes   795 g
1 (16 ounce) jar thick-
   and-chunky salsa   455 g
1 (15 ounce) can black
   beans, rinsed, drained   425 g
1 (15 ounce) can pinto
   beans, drained   425 g
1 (8 ounce) can whole
   kernel corn   230 g
1 tablespoon chili powder   15 ml
1 (8 ounce) package
   shredded cheddar
   cheese   230 g

- Combine tomatoes, salsa, black beans, pinto beans, corn and chili powder in large soup pot.

- Bring to boil, reduce heat and simmer for 15 minutes and stir often.

- Before serving, sprinkle 2 to 3 tablespoons (15 to 20 g) cheese over top of each serving. Serves 6.

Slow Cooker Soups & Stews

Soup, stew, chili and chowder recipes for your slow cooker so you can come home to great taste.

Slow Cooker Soups & Stews Contents

Slow Cooker Soups & Stews Contents

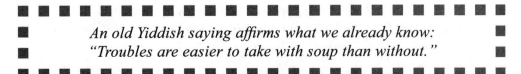

*An old Yiddish saying affirms what we already know:
"Troubles are easier to take with soup than without."*

Tasty Chicken and Rice Soup

1 pound boneless, skinless chicken breast halves	**455 g**
½ cup brown rice	**95 g**
1 (10 ounce) can cream of chicken soup	**280 g**
1 (10 ounce) can cream of celery soup	**280 g**
1 (14 ounce) can chicken broth with roasted garlic	**400 g**
1 (16 ounce) package frozen, sliced carrots, thawed	**455 g**
1 cup half-and-half cream	**250 ml**

- Cut chicken into 1-inch (2.5 cm) pieces. Place pieces in sprayed 4 or 5-quart (4 to 5 L) slow cooker.

- Mix rice, both soups, chicken broth and carrots in saucepan, heat just enough to mix well and pour over chicken.

- Cover and cook on LOW for 7 to 8 hours.

- Turn heat to HIGH, add half-and-half cream and cook for additional 15 to 20 minutes. Serves 6.

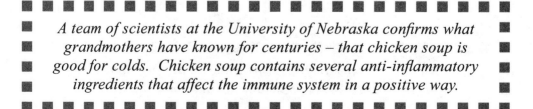

A team of scientists at the University of Nebraska confirms what grandmothers have known for centuries – that chicken soup is good for colds. Chicken soup contains several anti-inflammatory ingredients that affect the immune system in a positive way.

Chicken and Rice Soup

1 (6 ounce) package
long grain-wild
rice mix   170 g
1 (1 ounce) packet
chicken-noodle
soup mix   30 g
2 (10 ounce) cans
cream of chicken
soup   2 (280 g)
2 ribs celery, chopped
2 cups cooked, cubed
chicken   280 g

- Combine all ingredients and about 6 cups (1.4 L) water in 5 to 6-quart (5 to 6 L) slow cooker. Stir soup to mix.

- Cover and cook on LOW for 2 to 3 hours. Serves 6.

Chicken and Barley Soup

1½ - 2 pounds
boneless, skinless
chicken thighs   680 - 910 g
1 (16 ounce) package
frozen stew
vegetables   455 g
1 (1 ounce) packet
dry vegetable
soup mix   30 g
1¼ cups pearl barley   250 g
2 (14 ounce) cans
chicken broth   2 (400 g)

- Combine all ingredients plus 1 teaspoon (5 ml) each of salt and pepper and 4 cups (1 L) water in large, sprayed slow cooker.

- Cover and cook on LOW for 5 to 6 hours or on HIGH for 3 hours. Serves 6.

Confetti Chicken Soup

1 pound boneless,
  skinless chicken
  thighs   455 g
1 (6 ounce) package
  chicken and
  herb-flavored rice   170 g
3 (14 ounce) cans
  chicken broth   3 (400 g)
3 carrots, peeled,
  sliced
1 (10 ounce) can
  cream of chicken
  soup   280 g
1½ tablespoons
  chicken seasoning   20 g
1 (10 ounce) package
  frozen corn,
  thawed   280 g
1 (10 ounce) package
  frozen baby green
  peas, thawed   280 g

- Cut thighs in thin strips.

- Combine chicken, rice, chicken broth, carrots, soup, chicken seasoning and 1 cup (250 ml) water in 5 to 6-quart (5 to 6 L) slow cooker.

- Cover and cook on LOW for 8 to 9 hours.

- About 30 minutes before serving, turn heat to HIGH and add corn and peas to cooker.

- Continue cooking for additional 30 minutes. Serves 6.

Country Chicken Chowder

1½ pounds boneless,
skinless chicken
breast halves   680 g
2 tablespoons butter   30 g
2 (10 ounce) cans
cream of potato
soup   2 (280 g)
1 (14 ounce) can
chicken broth   400 g
1 (10 ounce) package
frozen corn   280 g
1 onion, sliced
2 ribs celery, sliced
1 (10 ounce) package
frozen peas and
carrots, thawed   280 g
½ teaspoon dried
thyme leaves   2 ml
½ cup half-and-half
cream   125 ml

- Cut chicken into 1-inch (2.5 cm) strips.

- Brown chicken strips in butter in skillet and transfer to large sprayed slow cooker.

- Add soup, broth, corn, onion, celery, peas and carrots and thyme to saucepan and heat just enough to mix well. Pour into cooker.

- Cover and cook on LOW for 3 to 4 hours or until vegetables are tender.

- Turn off heat, stir in half-and-half cream and set aside for about 10 minutes before serving. Serves 4 to 6.

Chicken-Pasta Soup

1½ pounds boneless, skinless chicken thighs, cubed	680 g
1 onion, chopped	
3 carrots, peeled, sliced	
½ cup halved pitted ripe olives	65 g
1 teaspoon minced garlic	5 ml
3 (14 ounce) cans chicken broth	3 (400 g)
1 (15 ounce) can Italian stewed tomatoes	425 g
1 teaspoon Italian seasoning	5 ml
½ cup small shell pasta	40 g
Parmesan cheese	

- Combine all ingredients, except shell pasta and parmesan cheese in saucepan and heat just enough to mix well. Pour into sprayed slow cooker.

- Cover and cook on LOW for 8 to 9 hours.

- About 30 minutes before serving, add pasta and stir.

- Increase heat to HIGH and cook for additional 20 to 30 minutes. Garnish with parmesan cheese. Serves 6.

Slow cookers work best when filled to between two-thirds and three-fourths of capacity.

Tortellini Soup

1 (1 ounce) packet white sauce mix	30 g
3 boneless, skinless chicken breast halves	
1 (14 ounce) can chicken broth	400 g
1 teaspoon minced garlic	5 ml
½ teaspoon dried basil	2 ml
½ teaspoon dried oregano	2 ml
½ teaspoon cayenne pepper	2 ml
1 (8 ounce) package cheese tortellini	230 g
1½ cups half-and-half cream	375 ml
1 (10 ounce) package fresh baby spinach	280 g

- Place white sauce mix in sprayed, 5 to 6-quart (5 to 6 L) slow cooker. Add 4 cups (1 L) water and stir until mixture is smooth.

- Cut chicken into 1-inch (2.5 cm) pieces.

- Add chicken, broth, garlic, ½ teaspoon (2 ml) salt, basil, oregano and cayenne pepper to white sauce mixture.

- Cover and cook on LOW for 6 to 7 hours or on HIGH for 3 hours.

- Stir in tortellini, cover and cook 1 hour more on HIGH.

- Stir in half-and-half cream and fresh spinach and cook just enough for soup to get hot. Serves 6.

Creamy Chicken Soup

2 cups milk	500 ml
1 (7 ounce) package cheddar-broccoli soup starter	200 g
1 cup cooked, finely chopped chicken breasts	140 g
1 (10 ounce) package frozen green peas, thawed	280 g
Shredded cheddar cheese	

- Place 5 cups (1.2 L) water and milk in slow cooker. Set heat on HIGH until water and milk come to a boil.

- Stir contents of soup starter into hot water and milk and stir well.

- Add chopped chicken, green peas and a little salt and pepper.

- Cook on LOW for 2 to 3 hours.

- To serve, sprinkle cheddar cheese over each serving of soup. Serves 4.

Chicken Stew

4 large boneless, skinless chicken breasts, cubed	
3 medium potatoes, peeled, cubed	
1 (26 ounce) jar meatless spaghetti sauce	740 g
1 (15 ounce) can cut green beans, drained	425 g
1 (15 ounce) can whole kernel corn, drained	425 g
1 tablespoon chicken seasoning	15 ml

- Combine cubed chicken, potatoes, spaghetti sauce, green beans, corn, chicken seasoning and ¾ cup (175 ml) water in 5 to 6-quart (5 to 6 L) slow cooker.

- Cover and cook on LOW for 6 to 7 hours. Serves 8.

Chicken Stew over Biscuits

2 (1 ounce) packets
   chicken gravy mix 2 (30 g)
2 cups sliced celery   200 g
1 (10 ounce) package
   frozen sliced
   carrots, thawed   280 g
1 (10 ounce) package
   frozen green peas,
   thawed   280 g
1 teaspoon dried basil 5 ml
3 cups cooked, cubed
   chicken or turkey
   breasts   420 g
Buttermilk biscuits

- Combine gravy mix, 2 cups (500 ml) water, celery, carrots, peas, basil, cubed chicken and ¾ teaspoon (4 ml) each of salt and pepper in slow cooker.

- Cover and cook on LOW for 6 to 7 hours.

- Serve over baked refrigerated buttermilk biscuits. Serves 6 to 8.

TIP: If you like thick stew, mix 2 tablespoons (15 g) cornstarch with ¼ cup (60 ml) water and stir into chicken mixture. Cook for additional 30 minutes to thicken.

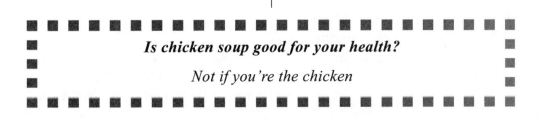

Is chicken soup good for your health?

Not if you're the chicken

Chicken-Tortellini Stew

1 (9 ounce) package
    cheese tortellini   255 g
2 small yellow
    squash, halved,
    sliced
1 red bell pepper,
    seeded, chopped
1 onion, chopped
2 (14 ounce) cans
    chicken broth   2 (400 g)
1 teaspoon dried
    rosemary   5 ml
½ teaspoon dried
    basil   2 ml
2 cups cooked,
    chopped chicken   280 g

- Place tortellini, squash, bell pepper and onion in slow cooker. Stir in broth, rosemary, basil and chicken.

- Cover and cook on LOW for 2 to 4 hours or until tortellini and vegetables are tender. Serves 6 to 8.

Celery-Chicken Chowder

3 cups cooked, cubed
    chicken   420 g
1 (14 ounce) can
    chicken broth   400 g
2 (10 ounce) cans
    cream of potato
    soup   2 (280 g)
1 large onion,
    chopped
3 ribs celery, sliced
    diagonally
1 (16 ounce) package
    frozen corn,
    thawed   455 g
⅔ cup whipping
    cream   150 ml

- Combine chicken, broth, potato soup, onion, celery, corn and ¾ cup (175 ml) water in 5 to 6-quart (5 to 6 L) slow cooker. Cover and cook on LOW for 3 to 4 hours.

- Add cream to slow cooker and heat for additional 15 minutes or until thoroughly hot. Serves 6.

Creamy Dreamy Turkey Soup

1 (8 ounce) carton fresh mushrooms	230 g
2 - 3 cups chopped cooked turkey breast	280 - 420 g
1 large onion, minced	
6 - 8 baby carrots, diced	
2 (10 ounce) cans cream of chicken soup	2 (280 g)
½ cup chicken broth	125 ml
1 (7 ounce) can green peas, drained	200 g
1 (4 ounce) jar diced pimentos, drained	115 g
½ cup milk	125 ml

- Clean mushrooms, remove stems and make 4 slices of each mushroom. Transfer to sprayed slow cooker.

- Add turkey, onion, carrots, soup and chicken broth and mix well.

- Cook on LOW for 7 to 8 hours or on HIGH for 3 to 4 hours.

- Add peas, pimentos and milk and stir well. Cook on LOW for additional 30 minutes or HIGH for 15 minutes. Serves 8.

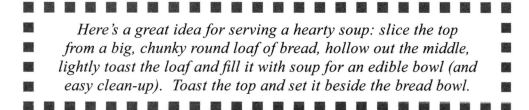

Here's a great idea for serving a hearty soup: slice the top from a big, chunky round loaf of bread, hollow out the middle, lightly toast the loaf and fill it with soup for an edible bowl (and easy clean-up). Toast the top and set it beside the bread bowl.

Turkey-Tortilla Soup

This is a great day-after-Thanksgiving meal.

2 (14 ounce) cans
   chicken broth   2 (400 g)
2 (15 ounce) cans
   Mexican stewed
   tomatoes   2 (425 g)
1 (16 ounce) package
   frozen succotash,
   thawed   455 g
2 teaspoons chili
   powder   10 ml
1 teaspoon dried
   cilantro   5 ml
2 cups crushed
   tortilla chips,
   divided   110 g
2½ cups chopped
   cooked turkey   350 g

- Combine broth, tomatoes, succotash, chili powder, cilantro, ⅓ cup (20 g) crushed tortilla chips and turkey in large slow cooker and stir well.

- Cover and cook on LOW for 3 to 5 hours.

- When ready to serve, sprinkle remaining chips over each serving. Serves 6.

TIP: Just to let you know, smoked turkey is just not as good as roasted turkey for this soup.

Turkey-Tortellini-Tomato Soup

1 (16 ounce) package
   turkey sausage   455 g
2 (15 ounce) cans
   Italian stewed
   tomatoes   2 (425 g)
1 (14 ounce) can
   chicken broth   400 g
2 (10 ounce) cans
   French onion soup   2 (280 g)
1 (12 ounce) package
   coleslaw mix   340 g
1 (9 ounce) package
   refrigerated
   cheese tortellini   255 g

- Brown and crumble turkey sausage in skillet, drain and place in large, sprayed slow cooker.

- Add tomatoes, chicken broth, onion soup, coleslaw mix and 2 cups (500 ml) water.

- Cover and cook on LOW heat for 5 to 6 hours.

- Turn heat to HIGH and add tortellini. Cover and cook for additional 20 minutes. Serves 6 to 8.

Andy Warhol said he painted soup cans because he had soup for lunch every day for 20 years.

Turkey-Mushroom Soup

Here's another great way to use leftover chicken or turkey.

2 cups sliced shitake mushrooms	145 g
2 ribs celery, sliced	
1 small onion, chopped	
2 tablespoons butter	30 g
1 (15 ounce) can sliced carrots, drained	425 g
2 (14 ounce) cans chicken broth	2 (400 g)
½ cup orzo pasta	40 g
2 cups cooked, chopped turkey (do not use smoked turkey)	280 g

- Saute mushrooms, celery and onion in butter in skillet.

- Transfer to slow cooker and add carrots, broth, orzo and turkey.

- Cover and cook on LOW for 2 to 3 hours or on HIGH for 1 to 2 hours. Serves 6.

TIP: Button mushrooms are fine for this recipe, too.

Do not use meats that are still frozen in slow cookers as they may not cook thoroughly; it is not a problem with frozen vegetables.

Turkey-Veggie Chili

1 pound ground turkey	455 g
Olive oil	
2 (15 ounce) cans pinto beans with liquid	2 (425 g)
1 (15 ounce) can great northern beans with liquid	425 g
1 (14 ounce) can chicken broth	400 g
2 (15 ounce) cans Mexican stewed tomatoes	2 (425 g)
1 (8 ounce) can whole kernel corn, drained	230 g
1 (16 ounce) package frozen chopped onions and bell peppers, thawed	455 g
2 teaspoons minced garlic	10 ml
2 teaspoons ground cumin	10 ml
½ cup elbow macaroni	55 g

- Cook and brown turkey in skillet with a little oil and place in large slow cooker.

- Add beans, broth, tomatoes, corn, onions and bell peppers, garlic, cumin and a little salt and stir well.

- Cover and cook on LOW for 4 to 5 hours.

- Stir in macaroni and continue cooking for about 15 minutes.

- Stir to make sure macaroni does not stick to cooker and cook for additional 15 minutes or until macaroni is tender. Serves 8.

TIP: If you want to get "fancy," top each serving with dab of sour cream or 1 tablespoon (15 ml) shredded cheddar cheese.

Beef and Barley Soup

1 pound lean ground
   beef   455 g
3 (14 ounce) cans
   beef broth   3 (400 g)
¾ cup quick-cooking
   barley   150 g
1 (16 ounce) package
   frozen chopped
   onions and bell
   peppers   455 g
3 cups sliced carrots 365 g
2 cups sliced celery   200 g

- Brown ground beef in skillet, drain and transfer to 5-quart (5 L) slow cooker.

- Add beef broth, barley, onions and bell peppers, carrots and celery.

- Cover and cook on LOW for 7 to 8 hours. Serves 4 to 6.

Beef-Black Bean Soup

1 pound lean ground
   beef   455 g
2 onions, chopped
2 cups sliced celery   200 g
2 (14 ounce) cans
   beef broth   2 (400 g)
1 (15 ounce) can
   Mexican stewed
   tomatoes   425 g
2 (15 ounce) cans
   black beans, rinsed,
   drained   2 (425 g)

- Brown beef in skillet until no longer pink. Place in sprayed 5 to 6-quart (5 to 6 L) slow cooker.

- Add onions, celery, broth, tomatoes, black beans, ¾ cup (175 ml) water and a little salt and pepper.

- Cover and cook on LOW for 6 to 7 hours or on HIGH for 3 hours 30 minutes. Serves 6.

TIP: *If you like zestier soup, add 1 teaspoon (5 ml) chili powder.*

Tasty Cabbage and Beef Soup

1 pound lean ground beef	455 g
1 (16 ounce) package coleslaw mix	455 g
1 (15 ounce) can cut green beans	425 g
1 (15 ounce) can whole kernel corn	425 g
2 (15 ounce) cans Italian stewed tomatoes	2 (425 g)
2 (14 ounce) cans beef broth	2 (400 g)
Cornbread	

- Brown ground beef in skillet, drain fat and place in large slow cooker.

- Add slaw mix, green beans, corn, tomatoes and beef broth and a little salt and pepper.

- Cover and cook on LOW for 7 to 8 hours. Serve with cornbread. Serves 6.

Saucy Cabbage Soup

1 pound lean ground beef	455 g
1 small head cabbage, chopped	
2 (15 ounce) cans jalapeno pinto beans with liquid	2 (425 g)
1 (15 ounce) can tomato sauce	425 g
1 (15 ounce) can Mexican stewed tomatoes	425 g
1 (14 ounce) can beef broth	400 g
2 teaspoons ground cumin	10 ml

- Brown ground beef in skillet, drain and place in sprayed 5 to 6-quart (5 to 6 L) slow cooker.

- Add cabbage, beans, tomato sauce, tomatoes, broth, cumin and 1 cup (250 ml) water and mix well.

- Cover and cook on LOW for 5 to 6 hours or until cabbage is tender. Serves 6.

Chili Soup

3 (15 ounce) cans chili
   with beans   3 (425 g)
1 (15 ounce) can
   whole kernel corn 425 g
1 (14 ounce) can beef
   broth   400 g
2 (15 ounce) cans
   Mexican stewed
   tomatoes   2 (425 g)
2 teaspoons ground
   cumin   10 ml
2 teaspoons chili
   powder   10 ml
Flour tortillas

- Combine chili, corn, broth, tomatoes, cumin, chili powder and 1 cup (250 ml) water in 5 to 6-quart (5 to 6 L) slow cooker.

- Cover and cook on LOW for 4 to 5 hours. Serve with warm, buttered flour tortillas. Serves 6.

Beef-Noodle Soup

1½ pounds lean
   ground beef   680 g
1 onion, chopped
2 (15 ounce) cans
   mixed vegetables 2 (425 g)
2 (15 ounce) cans
   Italian stewed
   tomatoes   2 (425 g)
2 (14 ounce) cans
   beef broth   2 (400 g)
1 teaspoon dried
   oregano   5 ml
1 (10 ounce) package
   medium egg
   noodles   280 g

- Brown and cook ground beef until no longer pink in skillet and transfer to slow cooker.

- Add onion, mixed vegetables, stewed tomatoes, beef broth and oregano. Cover and cook on LOW for 4 to 5 hours.

- Cook noodles according to package directions. Add noodles to slow cooker and cook for 20 minutes. Serves 6.

Enchilada Soup

1 pound lean ground
   beef, browned,
   drained   **455 g**
1 (15 ounce) can
   Mexican stewed
   tomatoes   **425 g**
1 (15 ounce) can
   pinto beans with
   liquid   **425 g**
1 (15 ounce) can
   whole kernel corn
   with liquid   **425 g**
1 onion, chopped
2 (10 ounce) cans
   enchilada sauce   **2 (280 g)**
1 (8 ounce) package
   shredded 4-cheese
   blend   **230 g**
Tortilla chips

- Combine beef, tomatoes, beans, corn, onion, enchilada sauce and 1 cup (250 ml) water in sprayed 5 to 6-quart (5 to 6 L) slow cooker and mix well.

- Cover and cook on LOW for 6 to 8 hours or on HIGH for 3 to 4 hours.

- Stir in shredded cheese. If desired, top each serving with a few crushed tortilla chips. Serves 6.

Keep the lid on slow cooker (unless recipe calls for stirring); the slow cooker can take as long as 20 minutes to regain the heat lost when the cover is removed. Do not cook without cover in place.

Mexican Meatball Soup

3 (14 ounce) cans beef broth	3 (400 g)
1 (16 ounce) jar hot salsa	455 g
1 (16 ounce) package frozen corn, thawed	455 g
1 (18 ounce) package frozen meatballs, thawed	510 g
1 teaspoon minced garlic	5 ml

- Combine all ingredients in slow cooker and stir well.

- Cover and cook on LOW for 4 to 7 hours. Serves 4 to 6.

Beefy Rice Soup

1 pound lean beef stew meat	455 g
1 (14 ounce) can beef broth	400 g
1 (7 ounce) box beef-flavored rice and vermicelli mix	200 g
1 (10 ounce) package frozen peas and carrots	280 g
2½ cups tomato juice	625 ml

- Sprinkle stew meat with pepper, brown in non-stick skillet, drain and place in large slow cooker.

- Add broth, rice and vermicelli mix, peas and carrots, tomato juice and 2 cups (500 ml) water.

- Cover and cook on LOW for 6 to 7 hours. Serves 6.

Meatball-Potato Soup

1 (32 ounce) package frozen meatballs, thawed	910 g
2 (15 ounce) cans stewed tomatoes	2 (425 g)
3 large potatoes, peeled, diced	
4 carrots, peeled, sliced	
2 medium onions, chopped	
2 (14 ounce) cans beef broth	2 (400 g)
2 tablespoons cornstarch	15 g

- Combine meatballs, tomatoes, potatoes, carrots, onions, beef broth, a little salt and pepper and 1 cup (250 ml) water in sprayed 6-quart (6 L) slow cooker.

- Cover and cook on LOW for 5 to 6 hours.

- Turn heat to HIGH. Combine cornstarch with ¼ cup (60 ml) water, pour into cooker and stir to mix well.

- Cook for additional 10 or 15 minutes or until slightly thick. Serves 8.

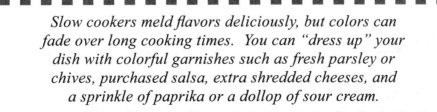

Slow cookers meld flavors deliciously, but colors can fade over long cooking times. You can "dress up" your dish with colorful garnishes such as fresh parsley or chives, purchased salsa, extra shredded cheeses, and a sprinkle of paprika or a dollop of sour cream.

Taco Soup Olé

2 pounds lean ground
   beef   **910 g**
2 (15 ounce) cans
   ranch-style beans
   with liquid   **2 (425 g)**
1 (15 ounce) can
   whole kernel corn,
   drained   **425 g**
2 (15 ounce) cans
   stewed tomatoes **2 (425 g)**
1 (10 ounce) can
   tomatoes and
   green chilies   **280 g**
1 (0.4 ounce) package
   ranch-style
   dressing mix   **10 g**
1 (1 ounce) packet taco
   seasoning mix   **30 g**

- Brown ground beef in large skillet, drain and transfer to slow cooker.

- Add 1 cup (250 ml) water and remaining ingredients and stir well.

- Cover and cook on LOW for 8 to 10 hours. Serves 8.

TIP: If you have some shredded cheddar cheese, it's fun to sprinkle some over each serving.

Need to thicken your soup? Adding a little pasta or mashed potato flakes is a great way to add bulk to your soup.

Taco Soup

1½ pounds lean ground
   beef   680 g
1 onion, chopped
1 (1 ounce) packet taco
   seasoning mix   30 g
1 (15 ounce) can whole
   kernel corn with
   liquid   425 g
1 (15 ounce) can pinto
   beans with liquid   425 g
1 (15 ounce) can stewed
   tomatoes with liquid   425 g
1 (14 ounce) can beef
   broth   400 g
Tortilla chips

- Combine beef and onion in large skillet, brown and drain. Transfer to slow cooker.

- Add taco seasoning, corn, beans, tomatoes, 1 cup (250 ml) water and broth and stir well.

- Cook on LOW for 3 to 4 hours. Serve with tortilla chips. Serves 6.

TIP: If you want a garnish, top each serving with a dollop of sour cream. If you don't want to wait 3 to 4 hours, put ingredients in a large soup pot. Bring to boil, reduce heat and simmer for 1 to 2 hours.

Camp Stew in Slow Cooker

1 pound lean ground beef	455 g
1 onion, chopped	
2 large potatoes, peeled, diced	
1 (15 ounce) can pinto beans	425 g
1 (15 ounce) can cream-style corn	425 g
1 (8 ounce) can whole kernel corn, drained	230 g
2 (12 ounce) cans white chicken meat with liquid	2 (340 g)
2 (15 ounce) cans stewed tomatoes	2 (425 g)
1 cup ketchup	270 g
2 tablespoons lemon juice	30 ml
1 tablespoon Worcestershire sauce	15 ml
1 teaspoon hot sauce	5 ml

- Brown and cook beef and onion in large skillet over medium heat and stir until beef crumbles and is no longer pink; drain.

- Layer potatoes, pinto beans, cooked beef, cream-style corn and remaining ingredients in 6-quart (6 L) slow cooker.

- Cover and cook on LOW for 8 hours or until potatoes are tender. Serves 8.

Hamburger Soup

2 pounds lean ground
   beef   910 g
2 (15 ounce) cans chili
   without beans   2 (425 g)
1 (16 ounce) package
   frozen mixed
   vegetables,
   thawed   455 g
3 (14 ounce) cans
   beef broth   3 (400 g)
2 (15 ounce) cans
   stewed tomatoes   2 (425 g)

- Brown ground beef until no longer pink in skillet and place in 6-quart (6 L) slow cooker.

- Add chili, vegetables, broth, tomatoes, 1 cup (250 ml) water and 1 teaspoon (5 ml) salt and stir well.

- Cover and cook on LOW for 6 to 7 hours. Serves 6 to 8.

Meatball-Veggie Stew

1 (18 ounce) package
   frozen meatballs,
   thawed   510 g
1 (16 ounce) package
   frozen stew vegetables 455 g
1 (15 ounce) can stewed
   tomatoes   425 g
1 (12 ounce) jar beef
   gravy   340 g
2 teaspoons crushed
   dried basil   10 ml

- Place meatballs and vegetables in 4 to 5-quart (4 to 5 L) slow cooker.

- Stir stewed tomatoes, gravy, basil, ½ teaspoon (2 ml) pepper and ½ cup (125 ml) water in bowl and mix well.

- Transfer to slow cooker. Cover and cook on LOW for 6 to 7 hours. Serves 6.

Taco-Chili Soup

2 pounds very lean stew
    meat   910 g
2 (15 ounce) cans
    Mexican stewed
    tomatoes   2 (425 g)
1 (1 ounce) packet
    taco seasoning mix 30 g
2 (15 ounce) cans
    pinto beans
    with liquid   2 (425 g)
1 (15 ounce) can
    whole kernel corn
    with liquid   425 g

- Cut large pieces of stew meat in half and brown in large skillet.

- Combine stew meat, tomatoes, taco seasoning, beans, corn and 1½ cups (375 ml) water in 4 or 5-quart (4 to 5 L) slow cooker.

- Cover and cook on LOW for 5 to 7 hours. Serves 8.

TIP: *If you are not into "spicy," use the regular stewed tomatoes instead of Mexican stewed tomatoes.*

Hearty Meatball Stew

1 (32 ounce) package
    frozen meatballs,
    thawed   910 g
2 (15 ounce) cans
    Italian stewed
    tomatoes   2 (425 g)
2 (14 ounce) cans
    beef broth   2 (400 g)
2 (15 ounce) cans
    new potatoes,
    drained   2 (425 g)
1 (16 ounce) package
    baby carrots   455 g
1 tablespoon beef
    seasoning   15 ml
Corn muffins

- Place meatballs, stewed tomatoes, beef broth, potatoes, carrots and beef seasoning in 6-quart (6 L) slow cooker.

- Cover and cook on LOW for 6 to 7 hours. Serve with corn muffins. Serves 8.

Comfort Stew

1½ pounds premium
     stew meat   680 g
2 (10 ounce) cans
     French onion soup 2 (280 g)
1 (10 ounce) can
     cream of onion
     soup   280 g
1 (10 ounce) can
     cream of celery
     soup   280 g
1 (16 ounce) package
     frozen stew
     vegetables, thawed 455 g

- Place stew meat in sprayed slow cooker.

- Combine all soups and mix well. Spread evenly over meat, but do not stir.

- Turn slow cooker to HIGH and cook just long enough for ingredients to get hot, about 15 minutes.

- Change heat setting to LOW, cover and cook for 7 hours.

- Add vegetables and cook for additional 1 hour. Serves 6 to 8.

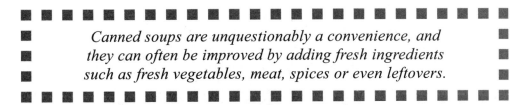

Canned soups are unquestionably a convenience, and
they can often be improved by adding fresh ingredients
such as fresh vegetables, meat, spices or even leftovers.

Gringo Stew Pot

1½ - 2 pounds lean
   beef stew meat   **680 - 910 g**
2 (15 ounce) cans
   pinto beans with
   liquid   **2 (425 g)**
1 onion, chopped
3 carrots, sliced
2 medium potatoes,
   peeled, cubed
1 (1 ounce) packet
   taco seasoning
   mix   **30 g**
2 (15 ounce) cans
   Mexican stewed
   tomatoes   **2 (425 g)**

- Brown stew meat in non-stick skillet.

- Combine meat, pinto beans, onion, carrots, potatoes, taco seasoning and 2 cups (500 ml) water in large slow cooker.

- Cover and cook on LOW for 6 to 7 hours.

- Add stewed tomatoes and cook for additional 1 hour. Serves 6.

TIP: This is great served with warmed and buttered flour tortillas.

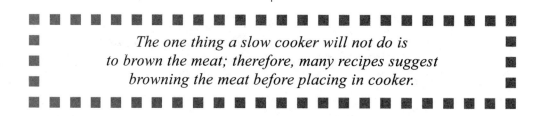

The one thing a slow cooker will not do is to brown the meat; therefore, many recipes suggest browning the meat before placing in cooker.

South-of-the-Border Beef Stew

1½ - 2 pounds
   boneless, beef
   chuck roast   680 - 910 g
1 green bell pepper,
   seeded
2 onions, coarsely
   chopped
2 (15 ounce) cans
   pinto beans with
   liquid   2 (425 g)
½ cup rice   50 g
1 (14 ounce) can
   beef broth   400 g
2 (15 ounce) cans
   Mexican stewed
   tomatoes   2 (425 g)
1 cup mild or medium
   green salsa   265 g
2 teaspoons ground
   cumin   10 ml
Flour tortillas

- Trim beef and cut into 1-inch (2.5 cm) cubes.

- Brown beef in large skillet and transfer to large sprayed slow cooker.

- Cut bell pepper into ½-inch (1.2 cm) slices.

- Add remaining ingredients with a little salt and 1½ cups (375 ml) water to slow cooker.

- Cover and cook on LOW for 7 to 8 hours.

- Serve with warm flour tortillas. Serves 8.

A Different Stew

2 pounds premium-cut stew meat	910 g
1 (16 ounce) package frozen Oriental stir-fry vegetables, thawed	455 g
1 (10 ounce) can beefy mushroom soup	280 g
1 (14 ounce) can beef broth	400 g
⅔ cup bottled sweet-and-sour sauce	180 g
1 tablespoon beef seasoning	15 ml

- Sprinkle stew meat with ½ teaspoon (2 ml) pepper, brown in skillet and transfer to slow cooker.

- Combine vegetables, soup, broth, sweet-and-sour sauce, beef seasoning and 1 cup (250 ml) water in bowl. Pour over stew meat and stir well.

- Cover and cook on LOW for 7 to 8 hours. Serves 8.

Roast and Vegetable Stew

3 cups roast beef, cooked, cubed	280 g
2 (15 ounce) cans stewed tomatoes	2 (425 g)
1 (16 ounce) package frozen mixed vegetables, thawed	455 g
2 (14 ounce) cans beef broth	2 (400 g)

- Combine all ingredients in 6-quart (6 L) slow cooker with a little salt and pepper. Cover and cook on LOW for 5 to 7 hours. Serves 6.

TIP: If you want some crunchy vegetables in your soup, add 1 cup (100 g) cauliflower florets and 1 cup (70 g) broccoli florets for about 1 hour before serving.

Hungarian Stew

2 pounds boneless short ribs	910 g
1 cup pearl barley	200 g
1 small onion, chopped	
1 green bell pepper, seeded, chopped	
1 teaspoon minced garlic	5 ml
2 (15 ounce) cans kidney beans, drained	2 (425 g)
2 (14 ounce) cans beef broth	2 (400 g)
1 tablespoon paprika	15 ml

- Combine all ingredients plus 1 cup (250 ml) water in slow cooker.

- Cover and cook on LOW for 8 to 9 hours or on HIGH for 4 hours 30 minutes to 5 hours. Serves 6.

Easy Chili

4 pounds lean ground beef	1.8 kg
2 (1 ounce) packages hot chili mix	2 (30 g)
1 (6 ounce) can tomato sauce	170 g
2 (15 ounce) cans stewed tomatoes with liquid	2 (425 g)
2½ teaspoons ground cumin	12 ml

- Break ground beef into pieces, brown in large skillet and drain. Use slotted spoon to drain fat and place beef in 5 to 6-quart (5 to 6 L) slow cooker.

- Add chili mix, tomato sauce, stewed tomatoes, cumin, 1 teaspoon (5 ml) salt and 1 cup (250 ml) water.

- Cover and cook on LOW setting for 4 to 5 hours. Serves 6.

TIP: If you think chili has to have beans, add 2 (15 ounce/425 g) cans ranch-style beans.

Chili Tonight

2 pounds lean beef chili
   meat   910 g
1 large onion, finely
   chopped
1 (10 ounce) can
   chopped tomatoes
   and green chilies   280 g
2½ cups tomato juice   625 ml
2 tablespoons chili
   powder   15 g
1 tablespoon ground
   cumin   15 ml
1 tablespoon minced
   garlic   15 ml

- Brown meat in skillet, drain and transfer to large slow cooker.

- Combine chili meat, onion, tomatoes and green chilies, tomato juice, chili powder, cumin, garlic and 1 cup (250 ml) water and mix well.

- Cover and cook on LOW for 7 to 8 hours. Serves 6.

Chunky Chili

2 pounds premium-cut
   stew meat   910 g
1 onion, chopped
2 (15 ounce) cans
   diced tomatoes   2 (425 g)
2 (15 ounce) cans
   pinto beans with
   liquid   2 (425 g)
1½ tablespoons
   chili powder   22 ml
2 teaspoons ground
   cumin   10 ml
1 teaspoon oregano   5 ml
Shredded cheddar
   cheese

- If stew meat is in fairly large chunks, cut each chunk in half. Brown in large skillet and transfer to large slow cooker.

- Add onion, tomatoes, beans, seasonings and a little salt.

- Cover and cook on LOW for 6 to 7 hours.

- Sprinkle shredded cheddar cheese over each serving. Serves 6.

Black Bean-Chile Soup

2 (14 ounce) cans chicken broth	2 (400 g)
3 (15 ounce) cans black beans, rinsed, drained	3 (425 g)
2 (10 ounce) cans tomatoes and green chilies	2 (280 g)
1 onion, chopped	
1 teaspoon ground cumin	5 ml
½ teaspoon dried thyme	2 ml
½ teaspoon dried oregano	2 ml
1 tablespoon minced garlic	15 ml
2 - 3 cups cooked, finely diced ham	280 - 420 g

- Combine chicken broth and black beans in slow cooker and cook on HIGH just long enough for ingredients to get hot.

- With potato masher, mash about half of beans in cooker.

- Reduce heat to LOW and add tomatoes and green chilies, onion, cumin, thyme, oregano, garlic, ham and ¾ cup (175 ml) water.

- Cover and cook for 5 to 6 hours. Serves 6.

Southern Soup

1½ cups dry
    black-eyed peas   185 g
2 - 3 cups cooked,
    cubed ham   280 - 420 g
1 (15 ounce) can
    whole kernel
    corn, drained   425 g
1 (10 ounce) package
    frozen cut okra,
    thawed   280 g
1 onion, chopped
1 large potato,
    peeled, cubed
2 teaspoons Cajun
    seasoning   10 ml
2 (14 ounce) can
    chicken broth   2 (400 g)
2 (15 ounce) cans
    Mexican stewed
    tomatoes   2 (425 g)

- Rinse peas and drain.

- Combine peas and 5 cups (1.2 L) water in large saucepan. Bring to boil, reduce heat and simmer for about 10 minutes.

- Drain peas and pour into 5 to 6-quart (5 to 6 L) slow cooker.

- Add ham, corn, okra, onion, potato, seasoning, broth and 2 cups (500 ml) water to slow cooker, cover and cook on LOW for 6 to 8 hours.

- Add stewed tomatoes and continue cooking for additional 1 hour. Serves 6.

Black-Eyed Pea Soup

5 slices thick-cut bacon, diced	
1 onion, chopped	
1 green bell pepper, seeded, chopped	
3 ribs celery, sliced	
3 (15 ounce) cans jalapeno black-eyed peas with liquid	**3 (425 g)**
2 (15 ounce) cans stewed tomatoes with liquid	**2 (425 g)**
1 teaspoon chicken seasoning	**5 ml**

- Cook bacon pieces until crisp in skillet, drain on paper towel and drop in slow cooker.

- With bacon drippings in skillet, saute onion and bell pepper, but do not brown.

- Transfer onions and bell pepper to slow cooker.

- Add celery, black-eyed peas, stewed tomatoes, 1½ cups (375 ml) water, 1 teaspoon (5 ml) salt and chicken seasoning.

- Cover and cook on LOW for 3 to 4 hours. Serves 6.

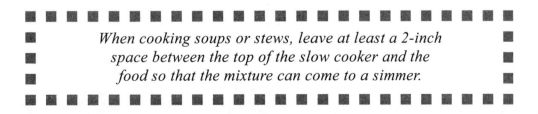

When cooking soups or stews, leave at least a 2-inch space between the top of the slow cooker and the food so that the mixture can come to a simmer.

Navy Bean-Bacon Soup

8 slices thick-cut
   bacon, divided
1 carrot, halved
   lengthwise, sliced
3 (15 ounce) cans
   navy beans
   with liquid   3 (425 g)
3 ribs celery,
   chopped
1 onion, chopped
2 (15 ounce) cans
   chicken broth   2 (425 g)
1 teaspoon Italian
   herb seasoning   5 ml
1 (10 ounce) can
   cream of chicken
   soup   280 g

- Cook bacon in skillet, drain and crumble.

- Combine half of crumbled bacon, carrot, beans, celery, onion, broth, scasoning and 1 cup (250 ml) water in 5 to 6-quart (5 to 6 L) slow cooker.

- Cover and cook on LOW for 5 to 6 hours.

- Ladle 2 cups (500 ml) soup mixture into blender and process until smooth.

- Return to cooker, add soup and stir to mix. Cook on HIGH for additional 10 to 15 minutes.

- Sprinkle remaining bacon crumbles on top of soup before serving. Serves 6.

Ham and Bean Soup

1 onion, finely chopped

2 ribs celery, chopped

2 teaspoons minced garlic — 10 ml

2 (14 ounce) cans chicken broth — 2 (400 g)

2 (15 ounce) cans pork and beans with liquid — 2 (425 g)

3 cups cooked, cubed ham — 420 g

⅓ cup pasta shells — 25 g

- Combine onion, celery, garlic, chicken broth, beans, ham and 1 cup (250 ml) water in 5 to 6-quart (5 to 6 L) slow cooker.

- Cover and cook on LOW for 4 to 5 hours.

- Turn cooker to HIGH heat, add pasta and cook for additional 35 to 45 minutes or until pasta is tender. Serves 6.

TIP: If you have time to fry some bacon, it's great crumbled on top of soup as garnish.

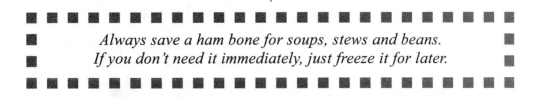

Always save a ham bone for soups, stews and beans.
If you don't need it immediately, just freeze it for later.

Cajun Bean Soup

1 (20 ounce) package
    Cajun-flavored,
    16-bean soup mix
    with flavor packet 570 g
2 cups cooked, finely
    chopped ham   280 g
1 onion, chopped
2 (15 ounce) cans
    stewed tomatoes   2 (425 g)
Cornbread

- Soak beans overnight in large slow cooker.

- After soaking, drain water and cover with 2 inches (5 cm) water over beans.

- Cover and cook on LOW for 5 to 6 hours or until beans are tender.

- Add ham, onion, stewed tomatoes and flavor packet in bean soup mix.

- Cook on HIGH for 30 to 45 minutes. Serve with cornbread. Serves 6.

Slow-Cook Navy Bean Soup

Better than Grandma's!

1½ cups dried navy beans 395 g
1 bell pepper, seeded,
    chopped
1 carrot, finely chopped
2 celery ribs, finely
    chopped
1 small onion, finely
    chopped
1 (1 pound) ham hock   455 g

- Soak beans for 8 to 12 hours and drain.

- Place all ingredients in 2-quart (2 L) slow cooker, add 5 cups (1.2 L) water and ½ teaspoon (2 ml) salt and a little pepper.

- Cook for 8 to 10 hours on LOW setting.

- Remove ham hock and discard skin, fat and bone.

- Cut meat in small pieces and place in soup. Beans can be mashed, if desired. Serves 4 to 6.

Pork and Hominy Soup

2 pounds pork
    shoulder, cubed   910 g
1 onion, chopped
2 ribs celery, sliced
2 (15 ounce) cans
    yellow hominy
    with liquid   2 (425 g)
2 (15 ounce) cans
    stewed tomatoes   2 (425 g)
2 (14 ounce) cans
    chicken broth   2 (400 g)
1 tablespoon ground
    cumin   15 ml
Tortillas
Shredded cheese
Green onions, chopped

- Sprinkle pork cubes with a little salt and pepper and brown in skillet. Place in 5 to 6-quart (5 to 6 L) slow cooker.

- Combine onion, celery, hominy, stewed tomatoes, broth, cumin and 1 cup (250 ml) water and pour over pork.

- Cover and cook on HIGH for 6 to 7 hours.

- Serve with warmed, buttered tortillas and top each bowl of soup with some shredded cheese and green onions. Serves 6.

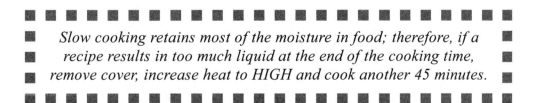

Slow cooking retains most of the moisture in food; therefore, if a recipe results in too much liquid at the end of the cooking time, remove cover, increase heat to HIGH and cook another 45 minutes.

Winter Minestrone

1 pound Italian
   sausage links,
   sliced   **455 g**
2 medium potatoes,
   peeled, cubed
2 medium fennel
   bulbs, trimmed,
   chopped
2½ cups peeled,
   chopped butternut
   or acorn squash   **600 ml**
1 onion, chopped
1 (15 ounce) can
   kidney beans,
   rinsed, drained   **425 g**
2 teaspoons minced
   garlic   **10 ml**
1 teaspoon Italian
   seasoning   **5 ml**
2 (14 ounce) cans
   chicken broth   **2 (400 g)**
1 cup dry white wine **250 ml**
1 (10 ounce) package
   fresh spinach,
   stems removed   **280 g**

- Cook sausage until brown in skillet and drain.

- Combine potatoes, fennel, squash, onion, beans, garlic and Italian seasoning in large slow cooker.

- Top with sausage and pour chicken broth and wine over all.

- Cover and cook on LOW for 7 to 9 hours.

- Stir in spinach, cover and cook for additional 10 minutes. Serves 8.

Tater Talk Soup

5 medium potatoes,
   peeled, cubed
2 cups cooked, cubed
   ham   280 g
1 cup chopped, fresh
   broccoli florets   70 g
1 (10 ounce) can
   cheddar cheese soup   280 g
1 (10 ounce) can fiesta
   nacho cheese soup   280 g
1 (14 ounce) can chicken
   broth   400 g
2½ soups can milk

- Place potatoes, ham and broccoli in sprayed slow cooker.

- Combine soups, broth and milk in saucepan and heat just enough to mix until smooth. Pour ingredients in slow cooker. Cover and cook on LOW for 7 to 8 hours. Serves 8.

Potato Soup

3 large potatoes, peeled, cubed
¼ cup (½ stick) butter,
   sliced   60 g
1 (14 ounce) can chicken
   broth   400 g
1 onion, finely chopped
2 cups milk   500 ml
2 cups cooked, cubed
   ham   280 g
1 (8 ounce) package
   cubed Velveeta®
   cheese   230 g
1 teaspoon dried parsley   5 ml
1 (8 ounce) carton
   whipping cream   250 ml

- Place potatoes, butter, broth, onion, milk and 2 cups (500 ml) water in sprayed 6-quart (6 L) slow cooker.

- Cook on HIGH for 30 minutes, reduce heat to LOW, cover and cook for 6 to 7 hours.

- Stir in ham, cheese, parsley and a little salt and pepper and cook on HIGH for 20 minutes or until cheese melts. Stir in whipping cream and serve hot. Serves 6.

Spicy Sausage Soup

1 pound mild bulk sausage	455 g
1 pound hot bulk sausage	455 g
2 (15 ounce) cans Mexican stewed tomatoes	2 (425 g)
3 cups chopped celery	305 g
1 (8 ounce) can sliced carrots, drained	230 g
1 (15 ounce) can cut green beans, drained	425 g
1 (14 ounce) can chicken broth	400 g

- Combine mild and hot sausage, shape into small balls and place in non-stick skillet.

- Brown thoroughly, drain and place in large slow cooker.

- Add remaining ingredients with 1 teaspoon (5 ml) salt and 1 cup (250 ml) water to slow cooker and stir gently so meatballs will not break up.

- Cover and cook on LOW for 6 to 7 hours. Serves 6.

Potato-Leek Soup

1 (1 ounce) packet white sauce mix	30 g
1 (28 ounce) package frozen hash-brown potatoes with onions and peppers, thawed	795 g
3 medium leeks, sliced	
3 cups cooked, cubed ham	420 g
1 (12 ounce) can evaporated milk	340 g
1 (8 ounce) carton sour cream	230 g

- Combine 3 cups (750 ml) water and white sauce in 4 to 5-quart (4 to 5 L) slow cooker and stir until smooth.

- Add potatoes, leeks, ham and evaporated milk. Cover and cook on LOW for 7 to 9 hours or on HIGH for 3 to 4 hours.

- When ready to serve, turn heat to HIGH and stir in sour cream. Cover and continue cooking for 15 minutes or until mixture is thoroughly hot. Serves 8.

Most slow cooker users suggest "tasting" before serving in order to add any needed seasonings such as salt, pepper, lemon juice, herb blends, Worcestershire, etc.

Spicy Black Bean Soup

1 pound hot pork
   sausage   455 g
1 onion, chopped
2 (14 ounce) cans
   chicken broth   2 (400 g)
2 (15 ounce) cans
   Mexican stewed
   tomatoes   2 (425 g)
1 green bell pepper,
   seeded, chopped
2 (15 ounce) cans
   black beans,
   rinsed, drained   2 (425 g)

- Break up sausage and brown with onion in large skillet. Drain fat and transfer to large slow cooker.

- Add chicken broth, stewed tomatoes, bell pepper, black beans and 1 cup (250 ml) water.

- Cover and cook on LOW for 3 to 4 hours. Serves 6.

Sausage Pizza Soup

1 (16 ounce) package
   Italian link
   sausage, sliced   455 g
1 onion, chopped
2 (4 ounce) cans sliced
   mushrooms   2 (115 g)
1 green bell pepper,
   seeded, julienned
1 (15 ounce) can
   Italian stewed
   tomatoes   425 g
1 (14 ounce) can
   beef broth   400 g
1 (8 ounce) can
   pizza sauce   230 g

- Combine all ingredients in slow cooker and stir well.

- Cover and cook on LOW for 4 to 5 hours. Serves 6.

Pork-Vegetable Stew

1 (1 pound) pork tenderloin	455 g
1 onion, coarsely chopped	
1 red bell pepper, seeded, julienned	
1 (16 ounce) package frozen stew vegetables, thawed	455 g
2 tablespoons flour	15 g
½ teaspoon dried rosemary leaves	2 ml
½ teaspoon oregano leaves	2 ml
1 (14 ounce) can chicken broth	400 g
1 (6 ounce) box long grain-wild rice	170 g

- Cut tenderloin into 1-inch (2.5 cm) cubes and brown in non-stick skillet.

- Place tenderloin in large sprayed slow cooker; add onion, bell pepper and mixed vegetables.

- Stir flour, rosemary and oregano into ½ cup (125 ml) water in bowl and mix well. Pour this seasoning mixture and broth over vegetables.

- Cover and cook on LOW for 5 to 6 hours.

- When ready to serve, cook rice according to package directions.

- Serve pork and vegetables over rice. Serves 6.

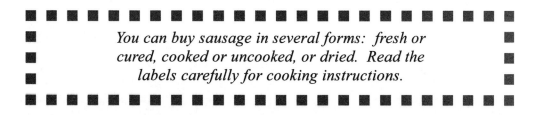

You can buy sausage in several forms: fresh or cured, cooked or uncooked, or dried. Read the labels carefully for cooking instructions.

Beans 'n Sausage Soup

**1 pound hot Italian
  sausage**   **455 g**
1 onion, chopped
**1 (15 ounce) can
  Italian stewed
  tomatoes**   **425 g**
**2 (5 ounce) cans
  black beans,
  rinsed, drained**   **2 (145 g)**
**2 (15 ounce) cans
  navy beans with
  liquid**   **2 (425 g)**
**2 (14 ounce) cans
  beef broth**   **2 (400 g)**
**1 teaspoon minced
  garlic**   **5 ml**
1 teaspoon dried basil 5 ml

- Cut sausage into ½-inch (1.2 cm) pieces.

- Brown sausage and onion in skillet, drain and transfer to 5 to 6-quart (5 to 6 L) slow cooker.

- Stir in tomatoes, black beans, navy beans, broth, garlic and basil and mix well.

- Cover and cook on LOW for 5 to 7 hours. Serves 6 to 8.

Italian Vegetable Stew

2 pounds Italian sausage	910 g
2 (16 ounce) packages frozen mixed vegetables	2 (455 g)
2 (15 ounce) cans Italian stewed tomatoes	2 (425 g)
1 (14 ounce) can beef broth	1 (400 g)
1 teaspoon Italian seasoning	5 ml
½ cup pasta shells	40 g

- Brown sausage in skillet, cook for about 5 minutes and drain.

- Combine sausage, vegetables, stewed tomatoes, broth and Italian seasoning in 5 to 6-quart (5 to 6 L) slow cooker and mix well.

- Cover and cook on LOW for 3 to 5 hours.

- About 40 minutes before serving, add shells to stew in slow cooker and cook until they are tender. Serves 8.

Recipes for the slow cooker were developed to make preparation as easy as possible because "convenience products" such as seasoning mixes, sauce mixes, canned soups, etc. can be used in most recipes.

Southern Ham Stew

*This is a great meal and
it screams for cornbread.*

2 cups dried
   black-eyed peas   250 g
3 cups cooked, cubed
   ham   420 g
1 large onion,
   chopped
2 cups sliced celery   200 g
1 (15 ounce) can
   yellow hominy,
   drained   425 g
2 (15 ounce) cans
   stewed tomatoes   2 (425 g)
1 (14 ounce) can
   chicken broth   400 g
2 tablespoons
   cornstarch   15 g

- Rinse and drain dried black-eyed peas and place in saucepan.

- Cover peas with water, bring to boil and drain again.

- Place peas in large slow cooker and add 5 cups (1.2 L) water, ham, onion, celery, hominy, tomatoes and broth.

- Cover and cook on LOW for 7 to 9 hours.

- Mix cornstarch with ⅓ cup (75 ml) water in bowl, turn cooker to HIGH, pour in cornstarch mixture and stir well.

- Cook for about 10 minutes or until stew thickens.

- Add good amount of salt and pepper and stir well before serving. Serves 6 to 8.

TIP: If you would like a little spice in the stew, substitute Mexican stewed tomatoes for stewed tomatoes.

Ham-Vegetable Chowder

When you bake a big ham, always make sure you have plenty leftover for this recipe.

1 medium potato	
2 (10 ounce) cans cream of celery soup	2 (280 g)
1 (14 ounce) can chicken broth	400 g
3 cups cooked, finely diced ham	420 g
1 (15 ounce) can whole kernel corn	425 g
2 carrots, peeled, sliced	
1 onion, coarsely chopped	
1 teaspoon dried basil	5 ml
1 (10 ounce) package frozen broccoli florets	280 g

- Cut potato into 1-inch (2.5 cm) pieces.

- Combine all ingredients except broccoli florets with 1 teaspoon (5 ml) each of salt and pepper in large slow cooker.

- Cover and cook on LOW for 5 to 6 hours.

- Add broccoli and cook for additional 1 hour. Serves 8.

Ham and Cabbage Stew

2 (15 ounce) cans Italian stewed tomatoes	2 (425 g)
3 cups shredded cabbage	210 g
1 onion, chopped	
1 red bell pepper, seeded, chopped	
2 tablespoons butter	30 g
1 (14 ounce) can chicken broth	400 g
3 cups cooked, diced ham	420 g
Cornbread	

- Combine all ingredients plus ¾ teaspoon (4 ml) each of salt and pepper and 1 cup (250 ml) water in large slow cooker and mix well.

- Cover and cook on LOW for 5 to 7 hours. Great with cornbread. Serves 6.

Split Pea and Ham Chowder

1 medium potato, peeled	
3 cups cooked, cubed ham	420 g
1 (16 ounce) package dried split peas, rinsed	455 g
1 (11 ounce) can whole kernel corn with red and green peppers	310 g
1 (14 ounce) can chicken broth	400 g
2 carrots, sliced	
2 ribs celery, diagonally sliced	
1 tablespoon dried onion flakes	15 ml
1 teaspoon dried marjoram leaves	5 ml

- Cut potato into small cubes and place in sprayed slow cooker.

- Combine all ingredients plus 3 cups (750 ml) water and 1 teaspoon (5 ml) salt in slow cooker.

- Cover and cook on LOW for 6 to 8 hours. Serves 6 to 8.

Shrimp and Chicken Jambalaya

4 boneless, skinless
    chicken breast
    halves, cubed
1 (28 ounce) can diced
    tomatoes   795 g
1 onion, chopped
1 green bell pepper,
    chopped
1 (14 ounce) can chicken
    broth   400 g
½ cup dry white wine   125 ml
2 teaspoons dried
    oregano   10 ml
2 teaspoons Cajun
    seasoning   10 ml
½ teaspoon cayenne
    pepper   2 ml
1 pound cooked, peeled,
    veined shrimp   455 g
2 cups cooked rice   370 g

- Place all ingredients except shrimp and rice in slow cooker and stir.

- Cover and cook on LOW for 6 to 8 hours.

- Turn heat to HIGH, stir in shrimp and rice and cook for additional 15 to 20 minutes. Serves 8.

Crab Chowder

2 small zucchini,
   thinly sliced
1 red bell pepper, seeded,
   julienned
2 ribs celery, diagonally
   sliced
1 medium potato,
   peeled, cubed
2 tablespoons butter,
   melted   30 g
1 (10 ounce) can
   chicken broth   280 g
2 tablespoons
   cornstarch   15 g
3 cups milk   750 ml
2 (6 ounce) cans
   crabmeat,
   drained, flaked 2 (170 g)
1 (3 ounce) package
   cream cheese,
   cubed   85 g

- Place zucchini, bell pepper, celery, potato, butter, broth and 1 teaspoon (5 ml) salt in sprayed slow cooker.

- Stir cornstarch into milk in bowl, stir and pour into slow cooker.

- Cover and cook on LOW for 3 to 4 hours.

- Turn heat to HIGH, add crabmeat and cream cheese and stir until cream cheese melts. Serves 6.

Oyster Chowder

1 red bell pepper, seeded, chopped	
1 onion, chopped	
1 (14 ounce) can chicken broth	425 g
1 medium potato, peeled, cubed	
1 fresh jalapeno pepper, finely chopped	
1 (8 ounce) carton shucked fresh oysters with liquor	230 g
1 (10 ounce) package frozen whole kernel corn, thawed	280 g
1 teaspoon dried oregano	5 ml
½ cup whipping cream	125 ml

- Combine all ingredients except cream in slow cooker.

- Cover and cook on LOW for 3 to 4 hours.

- When ready to serve, stir in cream. Serves 4 to 6.

Beans and Barley Soup

2 (15 ounce) cans pinto beans with liquid	2 (420 g)
3 (14 ounce) cans chicken broth	3 (400 g)
½ cup quick-cooking barley	100 g
1 (15 ounce) can Italian stewed tomatoes	425 g

- Combine beans, broth, barley, stewed tomatoes and ½ teaspoon (2 ml) pepper in 6-quart (6 L) slow cooker and stir well.

- Cover and cook on LOW for 4 to 5 hours. Serves 4 to 6.

Italian Bean Soup

2 (15 ounce) cans
great northern
beans with liquid   2 (425 g)
2 (15) ounce) cans
pinto beans with
liquid   2 (425 g)
1 large onion,
chopped
1 tablespoon instant
beef bouillon
granules   15 ml
1 tablespoon minced
garlic   15 ml
2 teaspoons Italian
seasoning   10 ml
2 (15 ounce) cans
Italian stewed
tomatoes   2 (425 g)
1 (15 ounce) can cut
green beans,
drained   425 g

- Combine both cans of beans, onion, beef bouillon, garlic, Italian seasoning and 2 cups (500 ml) water in large slow cooker.

- Cover and cook on LOW for 6 to 8 hours.

- Turn heat to HIGH, add stewed tomatoes and green beans and stir well.

- Continue cooking for additional 30 minutes or until green beans are tender. Serves 6 to 8.

TIP: Serve with crispy
*   Italian toast.*

French Onion Soup

5 - 6 sweet onions,
   thinly sliced
1 clove garlic, minced
2 tablespoons butter   30 g
2 (14 ounce) cans
   beef broth   2 (400 g)
2 teaspoons
   Worcestershire
   sauce   10 ml
6 (1 inch) slices
   French bread   6 (2.5 cm)
6 slices Swiss cheese

- Cook onions and garlic on low heat (do not brown) in hot butter in large skillet for about 20 minutes and stir several times.

- Transfer onion mixture to 4 to 5-quart (4 to 5 L) slow cooker.

- Add beef broth, Worcestershire sauce and 1 cup (250 ml) water.

- Cover and cook on LOW for 5 to 8 hours or on HIGH for 2 hours 30 minutes to 3 hours.

- Before serving soup, toast bread slices and place cheese slice on top.

- Broil for 3 to 4 minutes or until cheese is light brown and bubbles.

- Ladle soup into bowls and top with toast. Serves 6.

Delicious Broccoli-Cheese Soup

1 (16 ounce) package frozen
   chopped broccoli,
   thawed   455 g
1 (12 ounce) package
   cubed Velveeta®
   cheese   340 g
1 (1 ounce) packet white
   sauce mix   30 g
1 (1 ounce) packet dry
   vegetable soup mix 30 g
1 (12 ounce) can
   evaporated milk   340 g
1 (14 ounce) can chicken
   broth   400 g

- Combine all ingredients plus 2 cups (500 ml) water in large, sprayed slow cooker and stir well.

- Cover and cook on LOW for 6 to 7 hours or on HIGH for 3 hours 30 minutes to 4 hours.

- Stir 1 hour before serving time. Serves 6.

Cheesy Potato Soup

6 medium potatoes,
   peeled, cubed
1 onion, very finely
   chopped
2 (14 ounce) cans
   chicken broth   2 (400 g)
1 (8 ounce) package
   shredded
   American cheese 230 g
1 cup half-and-half
   cream   250 ml

- Combine potatoes, onion, chicken broth and ½ teaspoon (2 ml) pepper in slow cooker.

- Cover and cook on LOW for 8 to 10 hours.

- With potato masher, mash potatoes in slow cooker.

- About 1 hour before serving, stir in cheese and half-and-half cream and cook for additional 1 hour. Serves 6.

Pinto Bean-Vegetable Soup

4 (15 ounce) cans pinto beans with liquid	4 (425 g)
1 (16 ounce) package frozen chopped onions and peppers	455 g
2 cups chopped celery	200 g
2 (14 ounce) cans chicken broth	2 (400 g)
1 teaspoon Cajun seasoning	5 ml

- Place all ingredients plus 1 cup (250 ml) water in 5-quart (5 L) slow cooker and stir well.

- Cover and cook on LOW for 5 to 6 hours. Serves 6.

TIP: If you want to give this soup a little "kick," sprinkle a little cayenne or several drops of hot sauce. They will remember you that way.

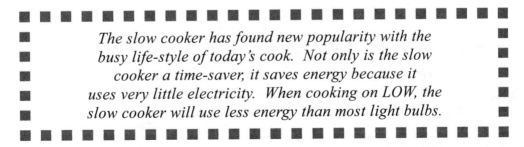

The slow cooker has found new popularity with the busy life-style of today's cook. Not only is the slow cooker a time-saver, it saves energy because it uses very little electricity. When cooking on LOW, the slow cooker will use less energy than most light bulbs.

Creamy Vegetable Soup

3 (14 ounce) cans chicken broth	3 (400 g)
¼ cup (½ stick) butter, melted	60 g
1 (16 ounce) package frozen mixed vegetables	455 g
1 onion, chopped	
3 ribs celery, sliced	
1 teaspoon ground cumin	5 ml
3 zucchini, coarsely chopped	
2 cups chopped, fresh broccoli	140 g
1 cup half-and-half cream	250 ml

- Combine broth, butter, mixed vegetables, onion, celery, cumin, 1 teaspoon (5 ml) each of salt and pepper in large slow cooker and stir well.

- Cover and cook on LOW for 6 to 7 hours or on HIGH for 3 to 4 hours.

- Stir in zucchini and broccoli. Cook for additional 30 minutes to 1 hour or until broccoli is tender-crisp.

- Turn off heat and stir in half-and-half cream.

- Let stand for 10 minutes before serving. Serves 6.

The first cookbook published in American in 1742 in Williamsburg, Virginia, contained recipes for Soop Sante, Pease Soop, Craw Fish Soop, Brooth, Soop with Teel, among others.

Pizza Soup

3 (10 ounce) cans
   tomato bisque
   soup   3 (280 g)
1 (10 ounce) can
   French onion soup 280 g
2 teaspoons Italian
   seasoning   10 ml
¾ cup tiny pasta
   shells   55 g
1½ cups shredded
   mozzarella cheese 70 g

- Place both soups, Italian seasoning and 1½ soup cans water in 4 to 5-quart (4 to 5 L) slow cooker.

- Cook for 1 hour on HIGH or until mixture is hot.

- Add pasta shells and cook for 1 hour 30 minutes to 2 hours or until pasta cooks. Stir several times to keep pasta from sticking to bottom of slow cooker.

- Turn heat off, add mozzarella cheese and stir until cheese melts. Serves 4.

TIP: If you want a special way to serve this soup, sprinkle some french-fried onions over top of each serving.

Soup with a Zip

2 (15 ounce) cans
  Mexican stewed
  tomatoes   2 (425 g)
2 (14 ounce) cans
  chicken broth   2 (400 g)
2 (10 ounce) cans
  chicken noodle
  soup   2 (280 g)
1 (15 ounce) can
  shoe-peg corn,
  drained   425 g
1 (15 ounce) can cut
  green beans,
  drained   425 g
Shredded
  pepper-Jack cheese

- Place all ingredients except cheese in 4 to 5-quart (4 to 5 L) slow cooker and mix well.

- Cover and cook on LOW for 2 to 3 hours.

- When ready to serve, sprinkle shredded cheese over each bowl of soup. Serves 6.

Minestrone Soup

2 (15 ounce) cans
  Italian stewed
  tomatoes   2 (425 g)
2 (16 ounce) packages
  frozen vegetables
  and pasta-
  seasoned sauce   2 (454 g)
3 (14 ounce) cans
  beef broth   3 (400 g)
2 ribs celery, chopped
2 potatoes, peeled,
  cubed
1 teaspoon Italian
  herb seasoning   5 ml
2 (15 ounce) cans
  kidney beans,
  rinsed, drained   2 (425 g)
2 teaspoons minced
  garlic   10 ml

- Combine all ingredients with 1 cup (250 ml) water in large sprayed slow cooker and mix well.

- Cover and cook on LOW for 4 to 6 hours. Serves 8.

Pasta-Veggie Soup

2 yellow squash, chopped	
2 zucchini, sliced	
1 (10 ounce) package frozen corn, thawed	280 g
1 red bell pepper, seeded, chopped	
1 (15 ounce) can stewed tomatoes	425 g
1 teaspoon Italian seasoning	5 ml
2 teaspoons dried oregano	10 ml
2 (14 ounce) cans beef broth	2 (400 g)
¾ cup small shell pasta	55 g

- Combine squash, zucchini, corn, bell pepper, tomatoes, Italian seasoning, oregano, beef broth and 2 cups (500 ml) water in 6-quart (6 L) slow cooker.

- Cover and cook on LOW for 6 to 7 hours.

- Add pasta shells and cook for additional 30 to 45 minutes or until pasta is tender. Serves 4 to 6.

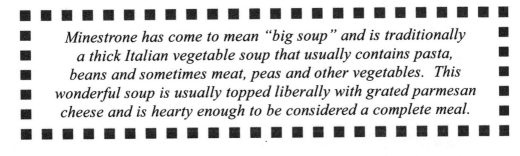

Minestrone has come to mean "big soup" and is traditionally a thick Italian vegetable soup that usually contains pasta, beans and sometimes meat, peas and other vegetables. This wonderful soup is usually topped liberally with grated parmesan cheese and is hearty enough to be considered a complete meal.

Vegetable-Lentil Soup

2 (19 ounce) cans
   lentil home-style
   soup   2 (550 g)
1 (15 ounce) can
   stewed tomatoes   425 g
1 (14 ounce) can
   chicken broth   400 g
1 onion, chopped
1 green bell pepper,
   chopped
3 ribs celery, sliced
1 carrot, halved,
   sliced
2 teaspoons minced
   garlic   10 ml
1 teaspoon dried
   marjoram leaves   5 ml

- Combine all ingredients in slow cooker and stir well.

- Cover and cook on LOW for 5 to 6 hours. Serves 4.

Vegetable Chili

2 (15 ounce) cans
   navy beans
   with liquid   2 (425 g)
1 (15 ounce) can
   pinto beans with
   liquid   425 g
2 (15 ounce) cans
   Mexican stewed
   tomatoes   2 (425 g)
1 (15 ounce) can
   whole kernel corn 425 g
1 onion, chopped
3 ribs celery, sliced
1 tablespoon chili
   powder   15 ml
2 teaspoons dried
   oregano leaves   10 ml

- Combine navy beans, pinto beans, tomatoes, corn, onion, celery, chili powder, oregano, 1 teaspoon (5 ml) salt and 1½ cups (375 ml) water in 5 to 6-quart (5 to 6 L) slow cooker.

- Cover and cook on LOW for 4 to 6 hours. Serves 6.

Serious Bean Stew

1 (16 ounce) package
smoked sausage
links 455 g
1 (28 ounce) can
baked beans with
liquid 795 g
1 (15 ounce) can
great northern
beans with liquid 425 g
1 (15 ounce) can pinto
beans with liquid 425 g
1 (10 ounce) can
French onion soup 280 g
1 onion, chopped
1 teaspoon Cajun
seasoning 5 ml
2 (15 ounce) cans
stewed tomatoes 2 (425 g)
Corn muffins

- Peel skin from sausage links and slice.

- Place in 6-quart (6 L) slow cooker, add remaining ingredients and stir to mix.

- Cover and cook on LOW for 3 to 4 hours.

- Serve with corn muffins. Serves 8.

Index

Cookbooks Published by
Cookbook Resources, LLC
Bringing Family and Friends to the Table

*The Best of Cooking
with 3 Ingredients*

*The Ultimate Cooking
with 4 Ingredients*

*Easy Cooking
with 5 Ingredients*

*Healthy Cooking
with 4 Ingredients*

*Gourmet Cooking
with 5 Ingredients*

*4-Ingredient Recipes
for 30-Minute Meals*

*Essential 3-4-5
Ingredient Recipes*

The Best 1001 Short, Easy Recipes

1001 Fast Easy Recipes

1001 Community Recipes

*Busy Woman's
Quick & Easy Recipes*

*Busy Woman's
Slow Cooker Recipes*

Easy Slow Cooker Cookbook

Easy One-Dish Meals

Easy Potluck Recipes

Easy Casseroles

Easy Desserts

Sunday Night Suppers

Easy Church Suppers

365 Easy Meals

365 Easy Chicken Recipes

365 Easy Soups and Stews

365 Easy Vegetarian Recipes

Quick Fixes with Cake Mixes

*Kitchen Keepsakes/
More Kitchen Keepsakes*

Gifts for the Cookie Jar

*All New Gifts
for the Cookie Jar*

Muffins In A Jar

The Big Bake Sale Cookbook

*Classic Tex-Mex
and Texas Cooking*

Classic Southwest Cooking

Miss Sadie's Southern Cooking

Texas Longhorn Cookbook

Cookbook 25 Years

A Little Taste of Texas

A Little Taste of Texas II

*Trophy Hunters'
Wild Game Cookbook*

Recipe Keeper

*Leaving Home Cookbook
and Survival Guide*

*Classic Pennsylvania
Dutch Cooking*

Easy Diabetic Recipes

www.cookbookresources.com

Your Ultimate Source for Easy Cookbooks

365 Easy Soup Recipes

Simple, Delicious Soups & Stews to Warm the Heart

cookbook resources® LLC

www.cookbookresources.com